THE
JAIN STUPA

THE
JAIN STUPA

AND
OTHER ANTIQUITIES OF MATHURA

BY

VINCENT A. SMITH,

INDIAN CIVIL SERVICE,

FELLOW OF THE ALLAHABAD UNIVERSITY

GYAN

Published by

Gyan Publishing House
5, Ansari Road
Daryaganj, New Delhi-110002
Phone: 011-47034999, 9811692060
E-mail: books@gyanbooks.com

Distribution Network
gyanbooks.com
India, USA, Canada, UK, Australia, France

ISBN : 978-81-212-2778-0 (HB)
First Published, 1901

2nd Impression 2021

Printed at: Gyan Press, Delhi.

The
Jain Stupa
Author: Vincent A. Smith

THE JAIN STÛPA

AND

OTHER ANTIQUITIES OF MATHURÂ.

BY

VINCENT A. SMITH,

INDIAN CIVIL SERVICE,

FELLOW OF THE ALLAHABAD UNIVERSITY.

ALLAHABAD:

Printed by FRANK LUKER, Superintendent, Government Press, North-Western Provinces and Oudh.

1901.

MATHURA.

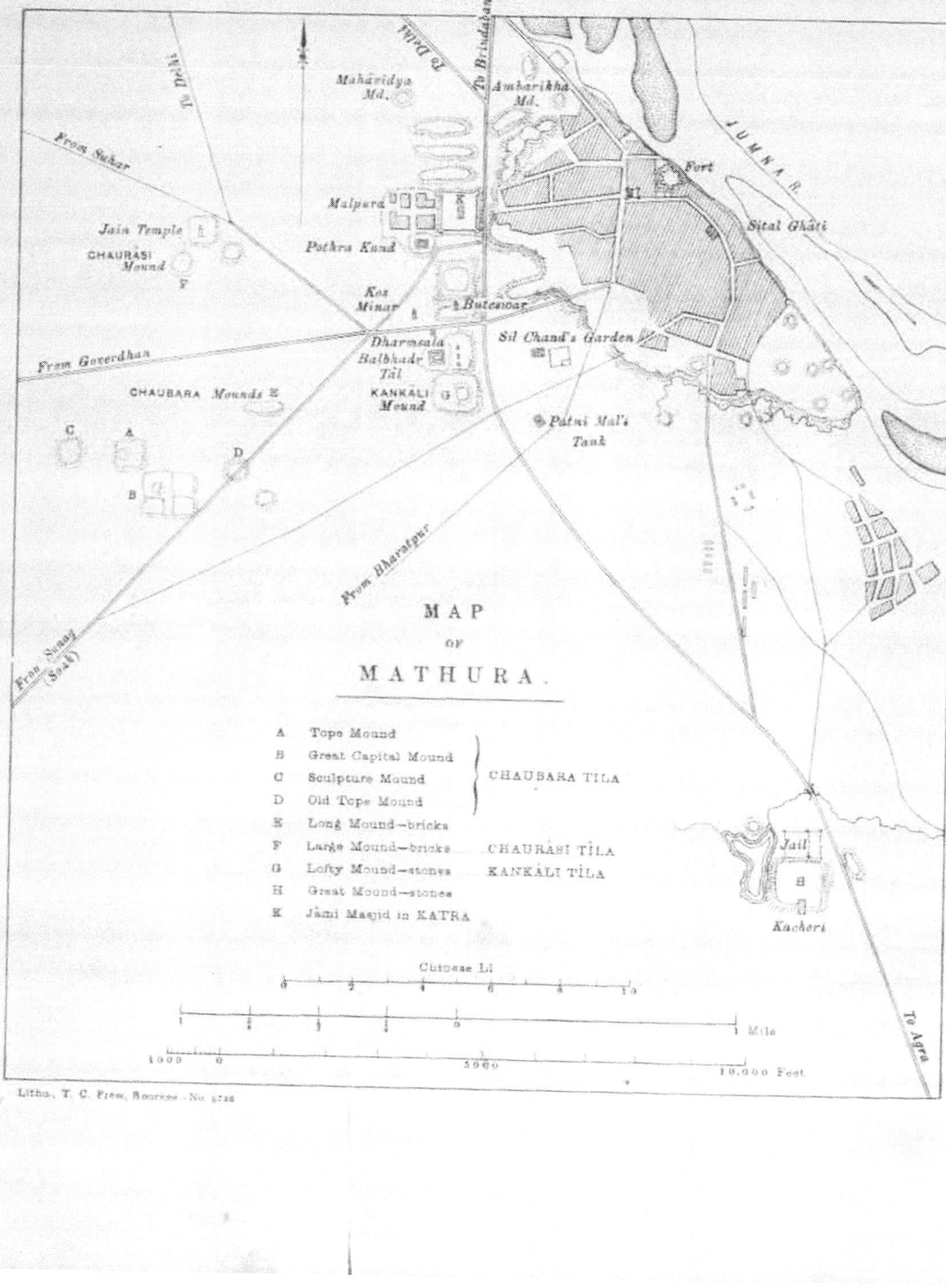

Litho., T. C. Press, Roorkee - No. 1786

List of volumes constituting the new Imperial Series of the Reports of the Archæological Survey of India.

Prescribed number in new Series.	Name of Book.	Author or editor.	Date (passed or proposed) of publication.	Provincial numbers. Western India.	Southern India.	Northern India.
I	Report of the first season's Operations in the Belgaum and Kaladgi Districts.	Burgess ...	1874 ...	I	...	.
II	Report on the Antiquities of Kathiawar and Kach.	Burgess ...	1876 ...	II	...	...
III	Report on the Antiquities of the Bidar and Aurangabad Districts.	Burgess ...	1878 ...	III	...	...
IV	The Buddhist Caves and their Inscriptions ...	Burgess ...	1883 ...	IV	...	...
V	The Caves of Elura and other Brahmanical and Jaina Caves in Western India.	Burgess ...	1884 ...	V	...	...
VI	The Buddhist Stupas of Amaravati and Jaggayyapeta.	Burgess ...	1887 ..	...	I	...
VII	List of Antiquarian Remains in the Presidency of Madras (Volume I).	Sewell ...	1882 ...	...	II	...
VIII	List of Inscriptions and Sketches of Dynasties of Southern India (Volume I).	Sewell ...	1884 ...	...	III	...
IX	South Indian Inscriptions (Volume I) ...	Hultzsch ...	1890 ...	...	IV	...
X	South Indian Inscriptions (Volume II) ...	Hultzsch ...	1891 ...	...	V	...
XI	Report on the Sharqi Architecture of Jaunpur.	Führer and Smith.	1889 ...	...	...	I
XII	Monumental Antiquities and Inscriptions in the North-Western Provinces and Oudh.	Führer ...	1891 ...	...	...	II
XIII	Epigraphia Indica of the Archæological Survey of India (Volume I).	Burgess ...	1891 ...	..	...	...
XIV	Epigraphia Indica of the Archæological Survey of India (Volume II).	Burgess ...	1893 ...	...	...	..
XV	South India Buddhist Antiquities ...	Rea ...	1894 ...	...	VI	...
XVI	Revised List of Antiquities, Bombay ...	Cousens ...	1897 ...	VIII	...	...
XVII	List of Architectural and Archæological Remains in Coorg.	Rea ...	1894 ...	...	VII	...
XVIII	Report on the Moghul Architecture of Fatehpur Sikri.	Smith ...	1895 ...	...	...	...
	Report on the Moghul Architecture of Fatehpur Sikri (Part II).	Smith ...	1896 ..			

List of Volumes constituting the new Imperial Series of the Reports of the Archæological Survey of India—(concluded.)

Prescribed number in new Series.	Name of Book.	Author or editor.	Date (passed or proposed) of publication.	Provincial numbers.		
				Western India.	Southern India.	Northern India.
XVIII	Report on the Moghul Architecture of Fateh-pur Sikri (Part III).	Smith ...	1897 ...	...	...	III
	Report on the Moghul Architecture of Fateh-pur Sikri (Part IV).	Smith ...	1898 ...			
XIX	List of Monumental Antiquities and Inscriptions in the Central Provinces and Berar.	Cousens ...	1897 ...	...	...	IV
XX	The Jaina Stupa and some other Antiquities of Muttra.	V. A. Smith,	1901 ...	...	...	V
XXI	Chalukyan Architecture including examples from the Ballari District in Madras.	Rea ...	1896 ...	...	VIII	...
XXII	Bower Manuscript	Hœrnle ...	1894 ...	...	...	...
XXIII	Muhammadan Architecture of Gujrat ...	Burgess ...	1896 ...	VI	...	...
XXIV	The Muhammadan Architecture of Ahmed-abad.	Burgess ...	...	VII	...	...
XXV	Monumental Remains of the Dutch East India Company in the Presidency of Madras.	Rea ...	1897 ...	...	IX	...
*XXVI	...	...	...	...	...	VI
*XXVII	...	...	...	...	...	VII
*XXVIII	...	...	...	...	...	VIII
XXIX	South Indian Inscriptions (Volume III, Part I).	Hultzsch ...	1899 ...	...	X	...
XXX	Moghul Colour Decorations of Agra ...	Smith ...	1901 ...	...	...	IX
XXXI	List of Antiquarian Remains in His Highness the Nizam's Territory.	Cousens ...	1900 ...	...	...	...

* These numbers will be utilized for reports bearing on the same subject to which they were originally assigned [*vide* Government of India, Department of Revenue and Agriculture (Archæology and Epigraphy), No. 3672—42-6, dated the 10th October 1899].

PREFACE.

THE plates in this volume, excepting the frontispiece, Plate II*a*, and the supplementary plates, were prepared several years ago under the supervision of Dr. Führer, then Archæological Surveyor and Curator of the Lucknow Provincial Museum. When he quitted the service of Government in the autumn of 1898 he left the plates without a word of explanatory text, although a monograph on the Jain remains at Mathurâ had been advertised as in an advanced stage of preparation by him. Sir Antony MacDonnell, G.C.S.I., Lieutenant-Governor of the North-Western Provinces and Chief Commissioner of Oudh, consulted me as to the best way of utilizing the fine series of plates prepared by Dr. Führer. I advised that they should be published with a concise descriptive text, a short introduction, and references to any previous publications in which the subjects of them had been treated, no attempt being made to discuss the many questions of interest suggested by the plates. My recommendations were accepted, and, no one else being available to do the work, I undertook it. Any attempt to discuss at length the linguistic, palæographical, historical, artistic, and other topics connected with the works of art illustrated would have involved prolonged research, and resulted in a very bulky treatise. The plates and inscriptions have, therefore, been left to speak for themselves with only so much annotation and explanation as seemed indispensable.

In some cases I have been unable to accept as correct the headings affixed to the plates by Dr. Führer.

I am indebted in sundry matters of detail to notes prepared by Babu Puran Chandar Mukherji, who visited Mathurâ, and to some extent compared the plates with the originals in the Lucknow Museum. In a few cases he detected discrepancies between Dr. Führer's headings to the plates and the labels affixed to the originals in the Museum.

I have seen most of the originals from time to time, but official duties have prevented me from staying in Lucknow to make a minute examination of the objects described. Unfortunately no catalogue of the valuable Archæological collections in the Lucknow Museum exists. The collection is housed in a dark crypt and very inadequately displayed.

It is impossible for me to compile a thoroughly satisfactory work from materials collected by another man and left in an incomplete state. But, notwithstanding its admitted and obvious limitations and deficiencies, I believe that this book will be of great interest to Orientalists. In the spelling of Indian words I have followed the system adopted in the "Epigraphia Indica." The transliterations of the inscriptions are given in Roman characters. Nothing would, I think, be gained by the use of Nâgarî type.

V. A. SMITH.

GORAKHPUR:
February 1900.

CONTENTS.

		PAGE.
List of plates		i—iii
Introduction		1—6
Description of plates		7
Chapter	I.—Maps, views, and plans	*ib.*
Ditto	II.—The Arhat Nândyâvarta	12
Ditto	III.—*Âyâgapaṭas*, or Tablets of Homage	14
Ditto	IV.—Veneration of a *Stûpa*	22
Ditto	V.—Sculptured panels	24
Ditto	VI.—Naigamesha-Nemesa	25
Ditto	VII.—A *Toraṇa*	27
Ditto	VIII.—Decorative work	28
Ditto	IX.—*Toraṇa* pillars	29
Ditto	X.—Sundry carvings	30
Ditto	XI.—Decorative details	35
Ditto	XII.—Pillars and capitals	36
Ditto	XIII.—Railing pillars	37
Ditto	XIV.—Ornamental bosses on rail bars	39
Ditto	XV.—Coping stones and pediments	40
Ditto	XVI.—A seated saint	41
Ditto	XVII.—Sundry sculptures	42
Ditto	XVIII.—Quadruple Jain images	46
Ditto	XIX.—Vardhamâna	49
Ditto	XX.—Colossal Jain images	53
Ditto	XXI.—Rishabhanâth and Sarasvatî	55
Ditto	XXII.—Sundry sculptures	58
Ditto	XXIII.—Supplement	61

List of Plates.

Frontispiece.—Map of Mathurâ.

Plate		To face page.
I.—	Plan of the Kankâli mound	8
II.—	General view of the excavations	9
IIa.—	View of the excavations as in January 1889	ib.
III.—	Plan of the Jain *Stûpa*	10
IV.—	View of the Jain *Stûpa* as excavated	11
V.—	Section of the Jain *Stûpa*	ib.
VI.—	Base of Image of the Arhat Nândyâvarta, dated in the year 79	12
VII.—	*Âyâgapaṭa*, or Tablet of Homage, set up by Sihanâdika	14
VIII.—	Ditto ditto, an inhabitant of Mathurâ	15
IX.—	Ditto ditto of an unknown donor	16
X.—	Ditto ditto set up by the wife of Śivaghoshaka	17
XI.—	Ditto ditto, the wife of Bhadranadi	18
XII.—	Ditto ditto, Śivayaśâ	19
XIII.—	Ditto ditto, Sivamitrâ	20
XIV.—	Image of Âryavati, dated in the 42nd year of the Satrap Śodâsa	21
XV.—	Veneration of a *Stûpa*	22
XVI.—	*Gandharva* and *Suparṇas*	23
XVII.—	Sculptured panels	24
XVIII.—	Naigamesha-Nemesa	25
XIX.—	Obverse of *Toraṇa*	27
XX.—	Reverse ditto	ib.
XXI.—	Carved panel, deeply undercut	28
XXII.—	Ditto in low relief	ib.
XXIII.—	Umbrella of red sandstone	ib.
XXIV.—	Carved *Toraṇa* beam and string course	ib.
XXV.—	Ends of *Toraṇa* beams	ib.
XXVI.—	Carved door jamb	ib.
XXVII.—	Sculptured *Toraṇa* pillar	ib
XXVIII.—	Inscribed ditto	29
XXIX.—	Details of ornaments	ib.
XXX.—	Carved lintel	30
XXXI.—	Carved pediment and lintel	ib.
XXXII.—	Fragment of sculptured *Toraṇa*	ib.
XXXIII.—	Ditto	31
XXXIV.—	Bracket of *Toraṇa* beam	ib.
XXXV.—	Ditto	32
XXXVI.—	Fragments of sculptured brackets	ib.
XXXVII.—	Sculptured brackets	33
XXXVIII.—	Bases of small pillars	ib.
XXXVIIIa.—	Decorative details	34
XXXIX.—	Ditto	35
XL.—	Pinnacle of gateway	ib.
XLI.—	Perforated windows	ib.
XLII.—	Sculptured watercourses	ib.

	To face page.
XLIII.—Pillars	36
XLIV.— Do.	ib.
XLV.— Do.	ib.
XLVI.— Do.	ib.
XLVII.— Do.	ib.
XLVIII.— Do.	ib.
XLIX.—Capitals	ib.
L.—Capitals and pinnacle	ib.
LI.—Details of capitals	ib.
LII.—Railing pillars without human figures	37
LIII.— Ditto ditto	ib.
LIV.— Ditto ditto	ib.
LV.— Ditto ditto	ib.
LVI.— Ditto ditto	ib.
LVII.— Ditto ditto	ib.
LVIII.— Ditto ditto	ib.
LIX.— Ditto ditto	ib.
LX.—Railing pillar with human figures	38
LXI.— Ditto ditto	ib.
LXII.— Ditto ditto	ib.
LXIII.— Ditto ditto	ib.
LXIV.— Ditto ditto	ib.
LXV.—Ornamental bosses on rail bars	39
LXVI.— Ditto ditto	ib.
LXVII.— Ditto ditto	ib.
LXVIII.— Ditto ditto	ib.
LXIX.— Ditto ditto	ib.
LXX.— Ditto ditto	ib.
LXXI.— Ditto ditto	ib.
LXXII.— Ditto ditto	ib.
LXXIII.— Ditto ditto	ib.
LXXIV.— Ditto ditto	ib.
LXXV.— Ditto ditto	ib.
LXXVI.— Ditto ditto	ib.
LXXVII.—Details of coping stones of railings	40
LXXVIII.— Ditto ditto	ib.
LXXIX.— Ditto ditto	ib.
LXXX.— Ditto ditto	ib.
LXXXI.— Ditto ditto	ib.
LXXXII.— Ditto ditto	ib.
LXXXIII.— Ditto, and of a pedimnet	ib.
LXXXIV.— Ditto ditto	ib.
LXXXV.—A seated saint	41
LXXXVI.—Fragments of sculpture	42
LXXXVII.—Life-size headless statue	43
LXXXVIII.—Statue of a boy with aureole of flames	44
LXXXIX.—Statue of a royal personage	45

		To face page.
XC.—	Three quadruple images of Jain *Tirthaṁkaras*	46—48
XCI.—	Two images of Vardhamâna	49
XCII.—	Life-size image of a seated Jina	50
XCIII.—	Seated image of Vardhamâna	51
XCIV.—	Vardhamâna, surrounded by the previous 23 *Tirthaṁkaras*	52
XCV.—	Colossal image of a *Tirthaṁkara* dated 1038	53
XCVI.—	Ditto ditto 1134	*ib.*
XCVII.—	Pedestals of colossal Jain images ...	54
XCVIII.—	Image of Ṛishabhanâth, or Âdinâth, the first *Tirthaṁkara*	55
XCIX.—	Statues of Śarasvati and a female	56—57
C.—	Sculptured bracket of a *Toraṇa* beam	58
CI.—	Heads	59
CII.—	Double-faced rider on bull	60

Supplement.

CIII.—	Votive *Stûpa*	61
CIV.—	Ganeśa	62
CV.—	Buddhist capital	63
CVI.—	Ditto	*ib.*
CVII.—	Ditto	*ib.*

INTRODUCTION.

The Kankâlî, or Jaini, mound *(Tîlâ)*, from or near which most of the objects delineated in the plates of this work were excavated, stands in the angle between the Agra and Gobardhan roads, close to the south-west corner of the city of Mathurâ, and about half a mile south of the Katrâ. *(Frontispiece)*.

The name of the mound is derived from a modern temple, a mean shrine, which is occupied by an ancient carved pillar doing duty as a Hindu goddess, who has been dubbed Kankâlî. This temple stands about midway between the well and the Jain *Stûpa* which was excavated by Dr. Führer in the season 1890-91. The mound is nearly rectangular in shape and is approximately 500 feet long by 350 feet broad.[1] It long served as a quarry for bricks. Excavations for archæological purposes have been made at various dates. General Cunningham worked at the western end in March and November 1871; Mr. Growse operated on the northern portion in 1875, and Dr. Burgess and Dr. Führer extended the excavations to the eastern end at different times from 1887 to 1896. Mr. Harding, a predecessor of Mr. Growse as Magistrate of Mathurâ, also made some excavations. A grove of trees has recently been planted on what is left of the mound, which will probably not be further explored.

Mr. Growse and Mr. Harding discovered in or close to the Kankâlî mound (1) two colossal statues of Buddha, each 7½ feet high, supposed to be now in the Public Library at Allahabad; (2) several mutilated statues of finer stone and superior execution; (3) a large figure of an elephant, without its trunk, found in 1871 in a garden, with an inscription dated 39 in the reign of the Kushân King Huvishka;[2] (4) a square pillar with four naked Jinas, dated in the year 9 in the reign of the Kushân King Kanishka; and (5) a considerable number of other statues and sculptures. Mr. Growse notes that the ancient figures are carved in coarse red sandstone with Pâlî inscriptions. The mediæval figures are executed in much finer material, and the inscriptions are in Sanskrit in characters of the eleventh century A. D.[3]

The objects found by Cunningham were, with the exception of one ten-armed Brahmanical figure, all Jain. They included several colossal and life-size statues, both male and female, all more or less mutilated; many broken statues of the Jain hierarchs, several being inscribed; and at least six examples of the pillars of *Stûpa* railings.

The inscriptions included the following :—

Cunningham's Plate.	Date.	Remarks.
XIII No. 2	Samvat 5	On a Jain pedestal.
ib. „ 3	Do. 5	Ditto.
ib. „ 4	Do. 9	On a Jain pedestal (mentions name of Kanishka).
ib. „ 5	———	Mentions Kanishka.
ib. „ 6	Samvat 20	On a Jain figure.
ib. „ 7	Do. 22	———

[1] The dimensions as stated in the text accord with Mr. E. W. Smith's plan (Plate I). Cunningham ("Archæological Reports," III, 19) gives the dimensions as 400 feet by nearly 300 feet.

[2] Cunningham, "Archæological Reports," Vol. III, page 20, plate V.

[3] Growse "Mathurâ," 3rd ed. (1883), pages 116—118.

Cunningham's Plate.	Date.	Remarks.
XIV No. 9	Samvat 39	On elephant capital (mentions Huvishka).
ib. " 10	Do. 47	———
ib. " 15	Do. 48	———mentions Huvishka.
XV " 16	Do. 83	On pedestal of life-size naked statue (mentions Vâsudeva).
ib. " 18	Do. 87	On life-size naked figure (mentions Vâsudeva).
ib. " 19	Do. 90	———(Cunningham's reading is mostly wrong—see *Ep. Ind.*, II., 205).
ib. " 20	Do. 98	On naked standing figure (mentions Vâsudeva).

Miscellaneous antiquities from the Kankâli mound are figured by Cunningham in Volume III of the "Reports" as follows :—

Plate.	*Object.*
II	Amethyst.
V	Elephant capital.
VII	Railing-pillar, with nude dancing-girl and other scenes.
VIII	Railing pillars and bars.
XI, D	Mutilated male figure.
XII, A	Foliage ornament.

In Volume XVII of the "Reports" (page 111), Cunningham notes that in the season of 1881-82 he dug up many Jain figures, including one inscribed with the name of Vardhamâna, the last of the 24 Jain pontiffs or Tîrthamkaras. During the operations of the same season the Hellenistic group of Herakles strangling the Nemean lion (*ibid*, Plate XXX) was found "amongst the heaps of fragments lying about." No more exact description of the find-spot is given. Several railing-pillars with statues of dancing-girls in the collection at the Mathurâ Museum are figured in Plate XXXI of the same volume, without any indication of the find-spot of each. Unfortunately the collection in the Museum at Mathurâ has never been catalogued or properly arranged, and no record was kept of the spot where each object was found.

Cunningham's last visit to Mathurâ in the season of 1882-83 is the subject of some desultory notes in Volume XX of the "Reports." Plates III and IV in that volume illustrate a few curious sculptures in the local Museum. Plate IV, figure 1, represents a nude Jain saint preaching, with a Nâga on each side adoring him. This sculpture probably belonged to the Digambara temple of the Kankâlî mound.

When Cunningham paid his early visits to Mathurâ in 1853, 1860, and 1863, as described in Volume I of the "Reports," pages 231—244, the Kankâli mound had not been noticed.

Dr. Führer's principal explorations of the Kankâli mound were effected in the three seasons 1888-89, 1889-90, and 1890-91. The Provincial Museum Report for the year ending 31st March 1889 enumerates as received by the Museum the following Mathurâ antiquities, most of which seem to have come from the Kankâli mound or its immediate neighbourhood :—

"10 inscribed statues of several Śvetâmbara Jinas of the Indo-Scythian period, four inscriptions of which are most important for the history of the Jainas;

34 pieces of sculpture forming parts of a magnificent Śvetâmbara Jaina temple of the time of the Indo-Scythian king Huvishka;

a statue of Mahâvîranâtha surrounded by the remaining 23 Tîrthamkaras;[1]

two colossal statues of the Jina Padmaprâbhanâtha, dated Samvat 1036 and 1134, respectively;[2]

---

[1] *Post*, Plate XCIV.

[2] *Post*, Plates XCV, XCVI. *For* "1036" *read* "1038."

four basements of Jina statues, inscribed Samvat 1134;

six bases of Buddha statues inscribed and dated in the regnal years of the Indo-Scythian rulers Huvishka, Kanishka, and Vâsudeva;

an inscribed statue of the Bodhisattva Amogha Siddhârtha of the first century A. D.;

10 inscribed Buddhist statues of the Indo-Scythian period;

a colossal pillar with the life-size figure of a dancing-girl;

19 Buddhist railing pillars of various sizes and patterns;

16 cross-bars of Buddhist railings;

12 pieces of copings of Buddhist railings;

a richly sculptured door-jamb, 10 feet high, of a Buddha temple of the Indo-Scythian period;

a beautifully carved stone umbrella, four feet in diameter, of a Buddhist *Stûpa*;[1]

a four-faced lion capital of the time of the Andhras;

24 exquisitely sculptured panels, some of which are inscribed in characters of the Indo-Scythian period;

a large slab, inscribed in the so-called shell characters, excavated from the Kankâli Tîlâ at Mathurâ."

The work was continued during the season 1889-90 when the Jain *Stûpa* and the western Jain temple belonging to the Digambara sect were exposed: 80 images of Tîrthaṁkaras, 120 pieces of stone railings, many miscellaneous sculptures, and numerous inscriptions, of which 17 belong to the Indo-Scythian (Kushân) period, from the year 5 to the year 86, were exhumed.

The most fruitful work was done in 1890-91. In the Museum Report for that year Dr. Führer writes :—

"Liberal grants by the Local Government in the Public Works Department and the Museum Committee have enabled the Curator to finish the excavations of the Kankâli Tîlâ at Mathurâ during the cold season of 1890-91. The results of his work far surpass those of the previous two years, as the new finds form important additions to our knowledge of Indian history and art.

"He forwarded to the Museum 737 fine pieces of sculpture, comprising beautifully-finished panels, doorways, *Toraṇas*, columns, complete railings with copings and bars, statues of Tîrthaṁkaras, &c.

"Amongst these sculptures is one which apparently possesses very considerable archæological interest. It is a *Toraṇa* bearing a relief which represents a *Stûpa* worshipped by Centaurs and Harpies, or, as the Hindus would say, Kinnaras and Garudas or Suparnas.[2]

"Centaurs have been found on the Buddhist sculptures at Bharhut[3] and Gaya, while Mathurâ has furnished the Silenus groups and Hercules strangling the Nemean lion. This new find is a further addition to the monuments which prove the influence of Hellenistic art among the Hindus of the last centuries preceding our era.

"Sixty-two of these sculptures are inscribed, bearing dates varying from 150 B. C. to A. D. 1023. On a beautifully carved *Toraṇa* there is a brief dedication, written in an ancient Prakrit dialect and in characters which appear a little more archaic than those of Dhanabhuti's inscriptions on the gateway of the Bharhut *Stûpa*, dated in the reign of the Sungas, or about B. C. 150.[4]

A second inscription, incised in two lines on an oblong slab, gives us the name of the founder of one of the temples excavated last year. Its characters do not differ much from those used in the earliest dated inscriptions of the Indo-Scythic period. As two temples have been discovered under the Kankâli Tîlâ, the natural inference from these inscriptions would be that one of them was built before 150 B. C. and the other considerably later, about the beginning of our era. Unfortunately, another circumstance has come to light which requires a modification of this assumption. The Curator has found several sculptures which have been carved out of more ancient ones.

"Thus, a pilaster bearing an inscription in characters of the Indo-Scythic period has been cut out of the back of an ancient naked Jina. Again, there is a small statue with a similar inscription cut out of the back of a sculptured panel bearing on the obverse a rather archaic inscription. These facts prove that the Jainas of the Indo-Scythic period at Mathurâ used for their sculptures materials from an older temple. Hence the discovery of the *Toraṇa*, with its very archaic inscription, shows indeed that there was a Jaina temple in Mathurâ before B. C. 150.

[1] Probably the umbrella figured in Plate XXIII, *post*, which is 4½ feet in diameter.

[2] Plate XV, *post*.

[3] I am informed on good authority that the correct spelling of this name is Barhut.

[4] Probably Plate XII, *post*.

Another important document is incised on the left portion of the base of a large standing statue, recording that this statue of Ara Tîrthaṁkara was set up in Samvat 78 within the precincts of 'a *Stûpa* built by the gods,' *i.e.* the *Stûpa* was so ancient that at the time when the inscription was incised its origin had been forgotten. On the evidence of the characters, the date of the inscription may be referred with certainty to the Indo-Scythian era, and is equivalent to A. D. 156.[1] The *Stûpa* which was laid bare last year must therefore have been built several centuries before the beginning of the Christian era; for the name of its builders would assuredly have been known if it had been erected during the period when the Jainas of Mathurâ carefully kept record of their donations.

Another donative inscription, dated Samvat 1080, proves, like the two colossal images with the dates Samvats 1036 and 1134, found in 1889,[2] that these ancient temples were used by the Jainas during the greater part of the eleventh century, and that their destruction happened in very late times."

The Museum Report for the year ending on the 31st March 1896 describes some further finds close to the Kankâlî mound. Dr. Führer writes :—

"The Archæological Surveyor, North-Western Provinces and Oudh, forwarded 57 ornamental slabs of great finish and artistic merit and 15 inscribed bases of images of Tîrthaṁkaras, which formed part of an ancient Jaina *Stûpa*, dating from the second century B. C. These sculptures were found in the course of excavations carried out in the unexplored fields adjoining the Kankâlî Tîla at Muttra (Mathurâ), which mound in 1889-91 had furnished the valuable and comprehensive collection of Jaina antiquities exhibited in the Museum. Like the numerous inscriptions found in former years, the new documents contain a considerable number of names of Jaina monks, and give in many instances longer spiritual pedigrees. One inscription especially, dated Samvat 299, and inscribed on the base of a life-size statue of Arhat Mahâvîra possesses, in spite of the omission of the reigning king's name, a considerable interest, and, in all probability, indicates that the dates of the Kushana kings of Mathurâ must be interpreted otherwise than is usually done.[3] Hitherto the dates of the Kushanas have been taken to be years of the Śaka era of 78 A. D., supposed to have been established by king Kanishka; but on the strength of this inscription it would seem that the beginning of this northern era must fall in the first half of the first century B. C.

Dr. Führer from time to time sent to the late Dr. Bühler impressions and photographs of the inscriptions and sculptures discovered, a selection from which was published by Dr. Bühler in the "Epigraphia Indica." In Volume I of that publication in the articles entitled "New Jaina Inscriptions from Mathurâ" and "Further Jaina Inscriptions from Mathurâ" (pages 371—397) thirty-five inscriptions from the Kankâlî mound were admirably edited.

The article entitled "Further Jaina Inscriptions from Mathurâ," in Volume II (pages 195—211) gave forty-one additional documents, and the article entitled "Specimens of Jaina Sculptures from Mathurâ" (pages 311—323), illustrated by four plates, supplied valuable explanations of some of the most interesting sculptures.

These writings of Bühler have been freely quoted in the descriptions of the plates in this volume.

Although the necessarily restricted plan of this work precludes me from attempting any elaborate discussion of the numerous topics of interest suggested by the plates, a few words pointing out some of the most obvious lessons to be learned from the discoveries in the Kankâlî mound will help the reader to take an intelligent interest in the drawings.

The plates throw light, among other things, on the history of the Indian, or Brâhmî, alphabet, on the grammar and idiom of the Prâkṛit dialects, on the development of Indian art, on the political and social history of Northern India, and on the history, organization, and worship of the followers of the Jain religion.

[1] Plate VI, *post*. The correct date is 79, not 78. The era used is not known.

[2] The dates are 1038 and 1134. See Plates XCV and XCVI, *post*.

[3] This document is not included in this volume, and I have not seen it. Until the inscription said to be dated in the year 299 has been published, no inference from it can be safely drawn.

The exact date of the earlier sculptures must remain uncertain until the era used by the great Kushân kings, Kanishka, Huvishka, and Vâsudeva has been determined. That era may, perhaps, prove to be the same which is used in the Kharoshṭhî inscriptions from the neighbourhood of Peshâwar, and has been supposed to be either identical, or nearly coincident, with the era B. C. 57, known as the Mâlava or Vikramâditya era. The theory of Fergusson and Oldenberg that Kanishka founded the Śaka era of A. D. 78 is not now generally accepted, although M. Specht still supports it. M. Sylvain Lévi places the accession of Kanishka at about the Christian era. I am satisfied, having regard to the numismatic evidence that that event cannot be placed earlier than A. D. 30. Everyone is agreed that the Kushân era, which undoubtedly dates from the accession of Kanishka, cannot have begun later than A. D. 78, nor earlier than B. C. 57.[1]

The Mathurâ inscriptions dated in the undetermined era range certainly from the year 5 to the year 98.[2] The years 5 and 98, therefore, lie respectively between the limits of B. C. 52 and A. D. 83, and A. D. 41 and A. D. 176.[3] The latest inscription found is dated in V. S. 1134, or A. D. 1067. The documents may, consequently, be assumed to cover a period of nearly eleven centuries, from the beginning of the Christian era to the middle of the eleventh century A. D.

The undated inscriptions in Plates VII and X may be referred to as examples of early records dating probably from about a century before the beginning of the Christian era. Their linguistic and palæographical peculiarities have been commented on by Bühler.

The document reproduced in Plate XIV is dated in the year 42, which may be assumed as approximately equivalent to B. C. 15. It is of special interest as mentioning the great Satrap *(Mahâkshatrapa)* Śodâsa, and determining his date as soon as the era used by him shall have been determined. That era is probably distinct from the era used by the Kushân kings.

The artistic merit of many of the sculptures is apparent, although in some cases the drawings fail to do full justice to the originals. The deep undercutting of much of the ornament is specially noticeable. The existence of Hellenistic works of art at Mathurâ has been long known, the most conspicuous examples being the so-called Silenus groups, and the Herakles strangling the Nemean lion. In the plates of this work Hellenistic influence may, I think, be traced. It was probably the result of intercourse with the Alexandrian school, which delighted in marine monsters and fantastic decoration. The general design of decoration in panels like that reproduced in Plate VIII seems to me to be decidedly Hellenistic. Attention is also invited to the description of Plate XIX.

The vine shown on the left border of Plate X is certainly Hellenistic The sculpture is probably too early in date to be Græco-Roman.

The harpies and centaurs of Plates XV and XVI obviously resemble to some extent those familiar in Greek art, although it is possible that they were borrowed directly from Assyria or Babylonia. The winged lions of the capitals in Plates XLIII to XLVI seem to be certainly of Assyrian or Babylonian origin. Other features of the capitals are Persian. The sculptures taken as a whole, though thoroughly Indian in subject, and for the most part in treatment, undoubtedly show a considerable amount of adaptation of foreign ideas.

---

[1] An excellent and well-reasoned article by M. A. M. Boyer, "L' Époque de Kaniska" *(Journal Asiatique*, Mai-Juin, 1900, page 526) has been published during the passage of this work through the press. M. Boyer's opinion (page 578) is thus expressed ;—" Je crois donc raisonnable l'admettre avec l'opinion générale, tout en le [Kanishka] rejetant comme fondateur del'ère Śaka, qu'il commença de regner vers la fin du premier siècle après J. C." I am disposed to agree, and to place the accession of Kanishka about A. D. 60 or 65.

[2] Inscriptions dated 135 and 299 are also said to exist.

[3] See note, p. 46, *post*.

Bühler has emphasized the lesson taught by the Mathurâ discoveries that Indian art was not sectarian. All religions, Buddhist, Jain, and Brahmanical, used the art of their age and country, and all alike drew on a common store-house of symbolic and conventional devices. *Stûpas*, sacred trees, railings, wheels, and so forth, were available equally to the Jain, Buddhist, or orthodox Hindu as religious symbols or decorative elements.

The discoveries have to a very large extent supplied corroboration to the written Jain tradition, and they offer tangible incontrovertible proof of the antiquity of the Jain religion, and of its early existence very much in its present form. The series of twenty-four pontiffs *(Tîrthaṁkaras)*, each with his distinctive emblem, was evidently firmly believed in at the beginning of the Christian era.

The inscriptions are replete with information as to the organization of the Jain church in sections known as *gaṇa*, *kula*, and *śâkhâ*, and supply excellent illustrations of the Jain books. Both inscriptions and sculptures give interesting details proving the existence of Jain nuns, and the influential position in the Jain church occupied by women.

Dr. Führer ("Progress Report" for 1890-91, page 13) states that in all 110 Jain inscriptions were collected at Mathurâ.

Most of those found in 1889 came from the central temple in the mound.[1] The inscribed images dated V. S. 1038 and 1134 (Plates XCV and XCVI) are quoted by Dr. Führer as proving that this central temple belonged to the Śvêtambara sect, but I notice that the images are nude.

The finds of 1890, he says, chiefly come from the second Jain temple, which according to a Nâgarî inscription, was still in the hands of the Digambara sect as late as V. S. 1080, A. D. 1023.[2]

According to Dr. Führer the mound also contained remains of a Buddhist *vihâra* and of a Vaishṇava temple. Some of the sculptures depicted in this work may belong to Buddhist or Brahmanical buildings, but most of them are certainly Jain. A few of the objects illustrated seem to have been included by mistake in this collection, as they came, according to the labels affixed to them, from places in Mathurâ distant from the Kankâli mound. The supplementary plates are from photographs supplied by Mr. Mukherji.

[1] Babu P. C. Mukherji, who recently visited the spot, reports that it is now impossible to identify with certainty the site of either temple.

[2] This inscription has not been edited.

Description of Plates.

CHAPTER I.—MAPS, VIEWS, AND PLANS.

FRONTISPIECE—MAP OF MATHURÂ.

THIS map is a reproduction of Plate I in Volume III of Cunningham's "Archæological Survey Reports" and is the best available, though not, I believe, quite accurate. It shows the position of the principal mounds, but omits many of the smaller ones. Small mounds are numerous between the Kankâlî and the Chaubârâ ruins.

The references for Mathurâ in Cunningham's "Reports" are as follows :—

Volume	I,	Pages	231—244,	Plates	XXXIX, XL.
"	III,	"	13— 46,	"	I—XVI.
"	XI,	"	75.		
"	XVII,	"	107—112,	"	XXX, XXXI.
"	XX,	"	30— 39,	"	II—V.

Mr. Growse's excellent "Mathurâ, a District Memoir" (3rd edition, Government Press, Allahabad 1883), may also be consulted. A rough plan of the environs of the city faces page 106 of that work.

PLATE I.

PLAN OF THE KANKÂLÎ MOUND.

THIS plate, prepared by Mr. E. W. Smith and a native draughtsman, is of much less value than it would have been if accompanied by a key and description. It shows clearly the position of the Jain *Stûpa*, but it is impossible to make out from it the positions of the two Jain temples or of anything else of interest. The materials for preparing a key to the plate are not now in existence.

MATHURÂ SERIES.—KANKÂLÎ TÎLÂ. PLATE I.

GENERAL PLAN OF SITE EXCAVATED, SHOWING POSITION OF ANCIENT JAINA BRICK STUPA AND FOUNDATIONS OF TEMPLES, &c.

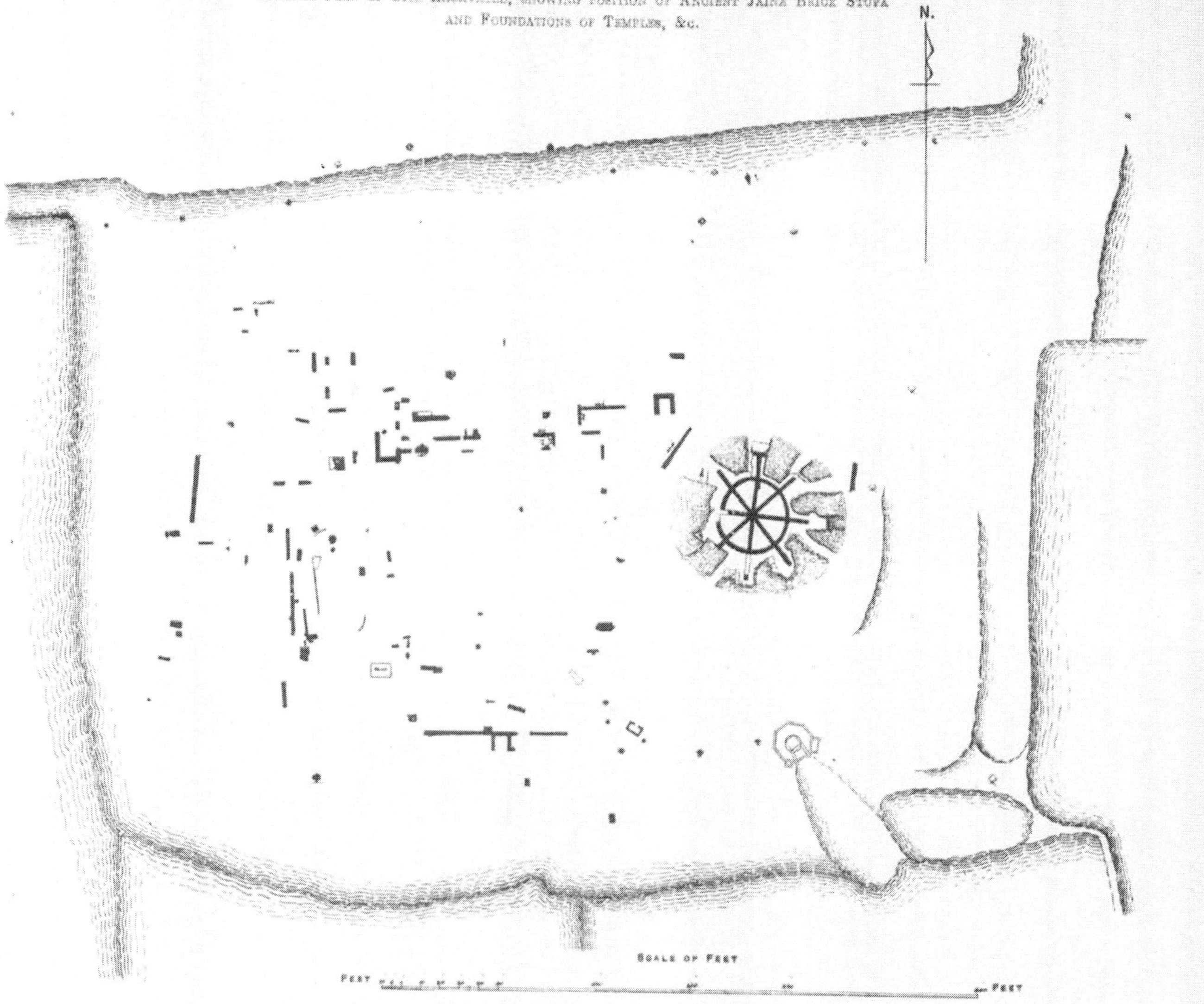

PLATE IIa.

MATHURA SERIES—KANKĀLĪ TĪLĀ.

General View of the Excavations in January 1889.

From a negative by Edmd. W. Smith.

Photo-etching-Survey of India Offices, Calcutta, August 18[illegible].

PLATE II.

GENERAL VIEW OF THE EXCAVATIONS.

PLATE II, in the absence of explanatory notes recorded at the time, is as unsatisfactory as Plate I, and I am unable to give the needed explanations.

Plate II*a*, from a photograph by a native artist, shows the state of the excavations in January 1889.

PLATE III.

PLAN OF THE JAIN *STÛPA*.

THIS plate gives an enlarged ground plan of the Jain *Stûpa*. The arrangement of radiating walls in the basement is merely a constructive device to save expensive masonry. The spaces between the radii were presumably filled in with clay. The devices used by *Stûpa* builders to attain the purpose of economizing masonry were very various. *Stûpas* of considerable size built throughout of solid masonry, like Mr. Peppé's Piprâhwâ *Stûpa* containing the relics of Buddha,[1] are rare.

[1] J. R. A. S. for July 1898, page 573.

MATHURÂ SERIES.—KANKÂLÎ TÎLÂ. PLATE III

PLAN OF ANCIENT JAINA BRICK STUPA EXCAVATED.

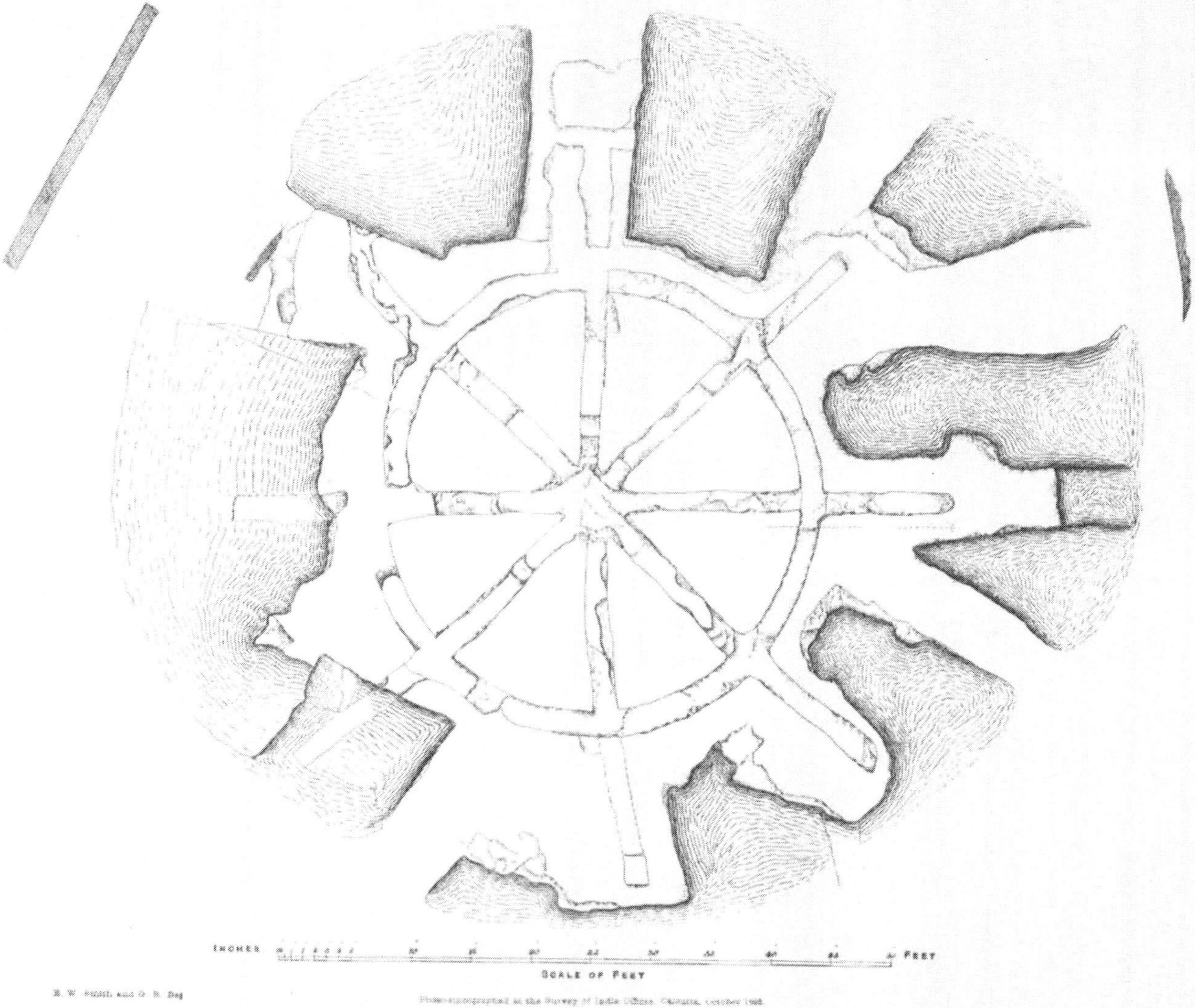

From a Negative by Edmd W. Smith.

Photo-etching—Survey of India Offices Calcutta, August 1896.

VIEW OF ANCIENT JAINA BRICK STÛPA EXCAVATED.

MATHURÂ SERIES.—KANKÂLÎ TÎLÂ.

CROSS-SECTION OF ANCIENT JAINA BRICK STUPA EXCAVATED.

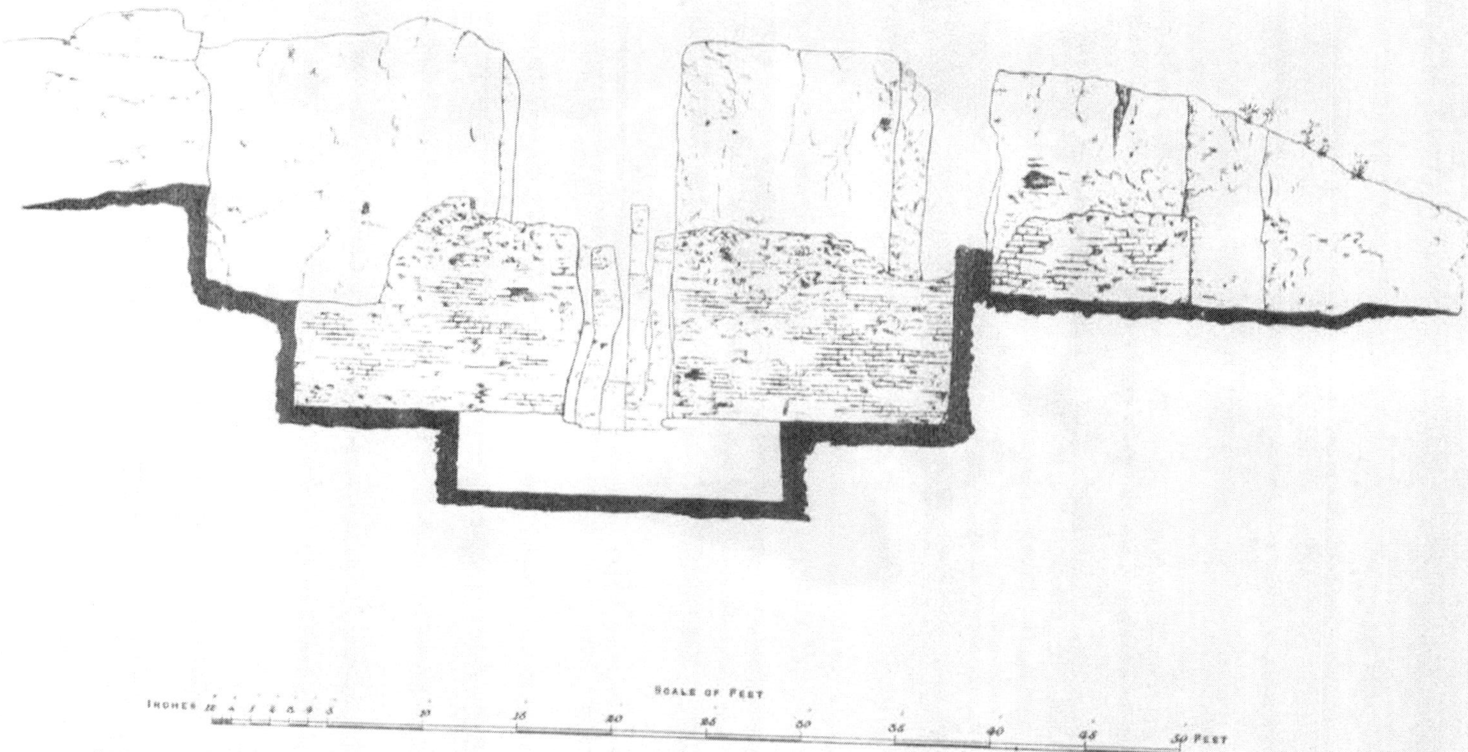

Hari Das Datta.

Photozincographed at the Survey of India Offices, Calcutta, October [illegible]

PLATES IV, V.

VIEW AND SECTION OF THE JAIN *STŪPA* AS EXCAVATED.

THESE plates add little to the information obtainable from the plan in Plate III.

Mr. Mukherji notes that the bricks brought to light during the excavations were of different sizes. Some were about 15 inches square and 6 inches thick, while others were long and comparatively narrow. The smallest bricks were about 7 inches broad and 2 inches thick. The smaller sizes were, naturally, better burnt than the larger sizes. In the remains of the ancient monastery at Sohnâg in the Gorakhpur District I have noticed a similar variation in the sizes of the bricks. The huge square slabs occur at Sohnâg also, and I measured one comparatively narrow brick there which was 19 inches long.[1]

[1] For a description of the great monastery at Sohnâg, see J. R. A. S. for July 1900.

CHAPTER II.—THE ARHAT NANDYAVARTA.

PLATE VI.

BASE OF IMAGE OF THE ARHAT NÂNDYÂVARTA, DATED IN THE YEAR 79.

THE subject of this plate is the left hand portion of the base of a large standing figure of a Jina found in the Kankâli mound in the season 1890-91. The other portion of the base has been lost.

The sacred symbol in the centre of the composition consists of a wheel resting on a *trisûl*, which is supported by a lotus flower. The group of worshippers on the right of the picture is formed of three women standing upright, and a little girl, who is partly hidden behind the stiff Assyrian-looking lion which crouches at the end of the slab. The lost portion was no doubt terminated by an exactly similar lion, and the group of worshippers on that side must have consisted of four male worshippers, of whom a portion of the figure of one remains. Each of the three women holds up in her right hand a long-stalked lotus flower.[1] The girl clasps her hands in an attitude of adoration. The dress of the women is peculiar and consists of a single long robe covering the whole body to the feet and confined at the waist. The inscription, though mutilated, is still intelligible, and is as follows :—

A. 1. *Saṁ LXX IX vr IV di XX*[2] *etasyâṁ purvvâyaṁ koṭṭiye gaṇe bairâyaṁ śâkhâyâṁ*

2. *ko Ayavridhahasti arahato Nandi* [*â*]*vartasa pratimaṁ nirvartayati*

B. . . . *bhâryyaye Śrâvikâye* [*dinâye*] *dânaṁ pratimâ Vodve thûpe devanirmite pra.*

"The year 79, the fourth (*month of the*) rainy season, the twentieth day, on that (*date, specified as*) above, Aya-Vṛidhahasti (*Arya-Vṛidhahastin*), a preacher in the Koṭṭiya *gaṇa* (and) in the Vaira *śâkhâ*, gave the advice to make an image of the Arhat Nandi âvarta (*Nândyâvarta*)[3] . . . . the image, the gift of the female lay-disciple Dinâ (Dattâ), wife of . . . . was set up at the Vodva *Stûpa*, built by the gods."[4]

The sculpture belongs to the Kushân period, and the mode in which the date is expressed shows that the year 79 must be referred to the era used by the great Kushân kings. This year 79 falls within the reign of Vâsudeva, one of whose inscriptions is expressly dated in the year 80.[5]

The character, language, and grammar of the Kushân inscriptions are discussed by Bühler in "Epigraphia Indica," Volume I, page 371 *seqq.*

The text of the inscription is of special interest as proving that *stûpas* were built by Jains[6] as well as Buddhists. The assumption has generally been made that all edifices in the *Stûpa* form are

---

[1] The object held by the woman nearest the symbol seems to be an opening bud; the objects held by the two other women are unmistakeable lotus flowers.

[2] The numerals 70, 9, 4, and 20 are each expressed in the ancient Indian manner by a single character. I use the Roman numerals as the nearest available equivalents. The *raḳm* notation used in Persian and Urdu accounts is similar in principle to the ancient Indian notation.

[3] Führer translates "the Arhat whose mark is the Nândyâvarta symbol," that is to say, Aranâtha, the 18th Tîrthaṁkara ("Progress Report" for 1891, page 16). He there gives the date as 78, but 79 is the correct reading. The Nândyâvarta is a complicated cross, somewhat resembling the *svastika*. We should expect to find this symbol on the base where the wheel is. Compare the wheel in Plate XCIII.

[4] Bühler, Ep. Ind., Vol. II, page 204, No. XX.

[5] I cannot attempt to discuss in this work the vexed question of the Kushân era (*ante*, p. 5). For the dated inscription of Vâsudeva see No. XXIV in "Epigraphia Indica," Vol. I, page 392.

[6] I purposely use the well-established English word Jain in preference to the pedantic Jaina, which is used by most of the recent writers on Indian antiquities.

PLATE VI.

MATHURÂ SERIES.—KANKÂLÎ TÎLÂ.

Base of Image of Arhat Nandyavarta, or Ara, dated Samvat 79, "set up at the Votva Stupa, built by the Gods".

Buddhist. When the inscription under discussion was executed, not later than A. D. 157 (79 + 78), the Vodva (Skr. Votva) *Stûpa* of the Jains at Mathurâ was already so ancient that it was regarded as the work of the gods. It was probably, therefore, erected several centuries before the Christian era, and may have been at least as ancient as the oldest Buddhist *Stûpa*. The record also gives interesting details of the internal constitution of the Jain church, the significance of which has been discussed by Bühler (*op. cit.*) and Führer.[1]

Bühler was fortunate enough to discover in the "Tîrthakalpa," or "Râjaprasâda" of Jinaprabha, a fourteenth century work based on ancient materials, the legend of the foundation and repair of this very "*Stûpa*, built by the gods."

According to this work, the *Stûpa* was originally of gold, adorned with precious stones, and was erected in honour of the seventh Jina, Suparśvanâth, by the goddess Kuberâ at the desire of two ascetics named Dharmaruchi and Dharmaghosha. In the time of the twenty-third Jina, Pârśvanâth, the golden *Stûpa* was encased in bricks, and a stone temple was built outside.

The sanctuary was restored in honour of Pârśvanâth by Bappa Bhaṭṭisûri, "thirteen hundred years after the lord Vira had reached perfection."[2]

Assuming the ordinarily received date, B. C. 527, for the death of Mahâvira to be correct, the attainment of perfection by that saint may be placed about B. C. 550. The restoration of the *Stûpa* may be dated about 1300 years later, or A. D. 750. Its original erection in brick in the time of Pârśvanâth, the predecessor of Mahâvira, would fall at a date not later than B. C. 600. Considering the significance of the phrase in the inscription "built by the gods" as indicating that the building at about the beginning of the Christian era was believed to date from a period of mythical antiquity, the date B. C. 600 for its first erection is not too early. Probably, therefore, this *Stûpa*, of which Dr. Führer exposed the foundations, is the oldest known building in India.

---

1 "Progress Report" for 1890-91, pp. 13—16.

2 "A Legend of the Jaina *Stûpa* at Mathurâ." ("*Sitzungsberichte der Kais Akademie der Wissenschaften in Wien*," 1897.)

CHAPTER III.—AYAGAPATAS OR TABLETS OF HOMAGE.

PLATE VII.

ÂYÂGAPAṬA, OR TABLET OF HOMAGE, SET UP BY SIHANÂDIKA.

Plates VII to XIII are devoted to the illustration of the very interesting and beautiful works technically known as *âyâgapaṭas.*

"An *Âyâgapaṭa* is an ornamental slab, bearing the representation of a Jina or of some other object of worship, and the term may be appropriately rendered by 'tablet of homage or of worship,' since such slabs were put up in temples, as the numerous inscriptions on them say, 'for the worship of the Arhats'. . . . . Among the Jainas they probably went out of fashion at an early period, as the inscriptions on them invariably show archaic characters, and are in no case known to me dated." [1]

Bühler was at first under the impression that the use of these highly decorated tablets was confined to the Jains; but Dr. Führer has recorded the discovery of a Buddhist example among the ruins of a Buddhist *vihâra* at Râmnagar in the Barelî district, the site of the ancient Adhichhattrâ or Ahichatra. That example is said to exhibit in the centre a fullblown lotus surrounded by four highly ornamented *triśûls*, and to bear an ancient inscription.[2]

The examples represented in the plates in this book are all Jain.

The central object in Plate VII is the seated figure of a Jina.

The surrounding carving comprises representations of pillars in the Persian Achæmenian style, and a great variety of sacred symbols, which I need not attempt to describe in detail. The workmanship is very fine.

The central figure has been reproduced as figure *a* of Plate I in "Epigraphia Indica," Volume II. The inscription is in characters of early form; probably anterior to the reign of Kanishka, and not later than the Christian era (*ibid.*, p. 197).

The text is as follows:—

L.—1. *Namo Arahantânaṁ Sihakasa Vânikasa putrena Kosikiputrena.*

2. *Sihanâdikena âyâgapaṭo pratithâpito Ârahaṁtapujâye.*

"Adoration to the Arhats! A tablet of homage (*âyâgapaṭa*) was set up by Sihanâdika (*Siṁhanadika? °nandika?*), son of the Vânika Sihaka (*Siṁhaka*) and son of a Kośiki (*Kauśiki mother*), for the worship of the Arhats."[3]

The term Vânika is supposed to be the name of the clan of Sihaka and his son Sihanâdika, who were probably Kshatriyas as indicated by the fact that the donor's mother was a Kauśikî.[4]

---

[1] "Epigraphia Indica," Vol. II, pp. 311, 314.

[2] "Epigraphia Indica," Vol. II, p. 314, Note 8. The Buddhist *âyâgapaṭa* does not appear to have been published.

[3] Professor Rhys Davids points out to me that the word *pûjâye* would be better translated "in honour of" than "for the worship of." The Arhats were not regarded as gods. But I have allowed Bühler's translations to stand unaltered.

[4] No. XXX in "Epigraphia Indica," Vol. II, p. 207.

MATHURA SERIES.—KANKÂLÎ TÎLÂ.

ÂYÂGAPATA, OR "TABLET OF HOMAGE OR OF WORSHIP," SET UP BY SIHANÂDIKA FOR THE WORSHIP OF THE ARHATS.

SCALE OF FEET

INCHES 12 9 6 3 FOOT

Photo-zincographed at the Survey of India Offices, Calcutta, October [illegible]

PLATE VIII.

MATHURÂ SERIES.—KANKÂLÎ TÎLÂ.

Âyâgapaṭa, or "Tablet of Homage," the Gift of an Inhabitant of Mathurâ.

Scale of Feet

Inches 12 9 6 3 0 1 Foot

PLATE VIII.

ÂYÂGAPAṬA, OR TABLET OF HOMAGE, SET UP BY AN INHABITANT OF MATHURÂ.

THIS fine work which is said to have been found north-east of the existing shrine of Kankâlî in March 1891, has for its central object a sacred wheel with sixteen spokes. The upper right corner has been lost. The bands of sculpture surrounding the wheel offer a rich variety of ornamental and symbolic designs.

The inscription is not visible in the plate, but the heading indicates that the archaic inscription No. VIII ("Epigraphia Indica," Volume II, pp. 200, 313) belongs to this slab.

The inscription is as follows :—

Namo arahato Mâhâvirasa Mâthuraka . . . lavâḍasa[sâ] . . . bhayâye . . . . va . . . itâye [âyâgapaṭo].

" Adoration to the Arhat Mahâvira *(Mahâvira)*. A tablet of homage *(âyâgapata, the gift)* of . . . itâ, the wife of . . . lavâḍa (?), an inhabitant of Mathurâ.

PLATE IX.

ÂYÂGAPAṬA, OR TABLET OF HOMAGE, OF AN UNKNOWN DONOR.

This tablet resembles that depicted in Plate VII in having for its central object the figure of a seated Jain saint. The surrounding symbolic ornaments, however, are quite different. Among them may be noticed the *svastika* or mystic cross, and a pair of fishes, omens of good luck, a second seated Jina (at the foot of the plate), a *Stûpa* (at the top of the plate), and sacred trees within railings (at the sides).[1] The slab thus offers another proof of the Jain veneration for *Stûpas*. The sacred trees closely resemble those generally associated with Buddhism. A photograph of this slab has been already published by Bühler, accompanied by an elaborate description. ("Epigraphia Indica," Volume II, Plate I, *b*, pp. 311–313). The remains of the inscription at the base are illegible.

[1] According to Dr. Führer, the eight auspicious marks of the Jains are: (1) the mystic cross (*Svastika*), (2) mirror (*Darpana*), (3) pot (*Kalasa*), (4) cane seat, shaped like an hour-glass (*Bhadrâsana*), (5, 6) two small fish, (7) flower garland, (8) book. ("Journal of Indian Art and Industry," October 1893, page 38.)

MATHURÂ SERIES.—KANKÂLÎ TÎLÂ.

Âyâgapaṭa, or "Tablet of Homage."

MATHURA SERIES.—KANKÂLÎ TÎLÂ

Âyâgapata, or "Tablet of Homage," set up by the Wife of Śivaghoshaka.

Photo-zincographed at the Survey of India Offices, Calcutta, October 1896.

PLATE X.

ÂYÂGAPAṬA, OR TABLET OF HOMAGE, SET UP BY THE WIFE OF ŚIVAGHOSHAKA.

A SEATED Jina occupies the centre of this tablet also, but in this case he has an attendant on each side. The symbolic ornaments are rather less rich and varied than in the examples previously described. The Jina in this case is unmistakeably Pârśvanâth, his head being canopied by his seven-hooded snake.

The inscription at the base is much mutilated. The characters are of an archaic type prior to the Kushân era. What is left of the record reads as follows :—

Namo arahaṁtânâ Sivagho[shaka]sa bhari[yâ] . . . . . . nâ . . . . . . nâ . . .

"Adoration to the Arhats . . . the wife of Śivaghoshaka." ("Epigraphia Indica," Vol. II, page 207 No. XXXI.)

The slab was found in January 1891.

PLATE XI.

ÂYÂGAPAṬA, OR TABLET OF HOMAGE, SET UP BY THE WIFE OF BHADRANADI.

THIS slab is said to have been found in December 1890 near the centre of the Kankâlî mound. It is not so well preserved as several of the other examples, and the drawing is, in consequence, not quite satisfactory. The central Jina cannot be identified. The ornaments include two massive pillars in a style quite different from those depicted in Plate VII *ante*. The inscription, which belongs approximately to the period of the great Kushân kings, is almost perfect, and is as follows :—

L. 1. *Namo Arahaṁtânaṁ[mala] ṣasa dhitu Bhadrayaśasa vadhuye Bhadranadisa bhayâye*

2. *A[chalâ]ye â[yâ]gapaṭo pratithâpito arahatapujâye.*

"Adoration to the Arhats! A tablet of homage (*Âyâgapaṭa*) was set up by Achalâ (?), daughter-in-law of Bhadrayaśa (*Bhadrayaśas*) and wife of Bhadranadi (*Bhadranandin*) for the worship of the Arhats." ("Epigraphia Indica," Volume II, page 207, No. XXXII.)

The plate seems to read Agolâ, rather than Achalâ, as read by Bühler with doubt.

MATHURA SERIES.—KANKÂLÎ TÎLÂ.

ÂYÂGAPATA, OR "TABLET OF HOMAGE," SET UP BY ACHALÂ, THE WIFE OF BHADRANADI.

Ram Pratap

SCALE OF FEET

INCHES 12" 9 6 3 1 FOOT

Photo-lithographed at the Survey of India Offices, Calcutta, October [illegible]

MATHURĀ SERIES.—KANKĀLĪ TĪLĀ.

Āyāgapaṭa, or "Tablet of Homage," the Gift of Śivayaśā, the Wife of the Dancer Phāguyaśa.

Scale

Inches 12 9 6 3 0 1 Foot

PLATE XII.

ĀYĀGAPAṬA OR TABLET OF HOMAGE SET UP BY ŚIVAYAŚĀ.

The upper part of the slab depicted in this plate has been lost. The lower and more important portion is well preserved, and the inscription is nearly complete.

The composition gives an interesting view of a Jain *Stûpa*, which was surrounded by a perambulation path guarded by a railing. The path is approached through a highly-decorated *Toraṇa* gateway, to which four steps ascend. A heavy wreath hangs from the lowest beam of the gateway. A dancing-girl, completely nude except for a sash round the hips and the usual jewellery, stands in an immodest attitude on the railing on each side of the gate. Two massive pillars with peculiar bases are shown, and a small portion of the railing surrounding an upper perambulation path is visible.

The general arrangements of the *Stûpa* are identical with those familiar to all students of Buddhist antiquities.

The railing is of a plain archaic type.

The characters of the inscription below the railing are in form anterior to the alphabet used by the Kushân kings, and may be considerably earlier than the Christian era. The inscription is as follows :—

L. 1 *a. Namo arahatânaṁ Phaguyaśasa*
2 *a. natakasa bhayâye Śivayaśâ*
3 *a. . . . i . . . . â . . . . â . . . . . . kâye*
1 *b. âyâgapato kârito*
2 *b. arahata pujâye.*

"Adoration to the Arhats! By Śivayaśâ *(Śivayaśas)*, wife of the dancer Phaguyaśa *(Phalguyaśas)* . . . . a tablet of homage *(âyâgapaṭa)* was caused to be made for the worship of the Arhats." ("Epigraphia Indica," Volume II, page 200, No. V.)

Mr. Mukherjî found an inscribed slab to the west of the bridge on the road leading to the Holi gate, containing a bas-relief representation of a *Stûpa* 10½ inches high,[1] which may be compared with the representation in this plate.

[1] *Post*, Plate CIII.

PLATE XIII.

ÂYÂGAPAṬA, OR TABLET OF HOMAGE, SET UP BY ŚIVAMITRÂ.

FIGURE 1 represents a fragment of an *âyâgapaṭa* of which more than half has been lost. The central object is among the parts missing. The ornaments include the lucky fish, which has been noticed in Plate VII, and beautifully executed flower and scroll designs. The slab was found by Dr. Burgess in 1887. The inscription at the base is in archaic characters apparently anterior to the Kushân period, and thus adds one more to the many proofs of the antiquity of the Jain worship at Mathurâ. The record, though incomplete, is sufficiently intelligible, and is as follows :—

L. 1. *Namo arahato Vardhamânasya Gotiputrasa Poṭhaya—Śaka* . . .
2. *Kâlavâḷasa*
3. . . . . *Kośikeye Śimitrâye âyâgapaṭo prati.*

"Adoration to the Arhat Vardhamâna! A tablet of homage was set up by Śivamitrâ *(of)* the Kauśika *(family)* (wife) of Gotiputra (*Gauptîputra*), a black serpent for the Poṭhayas and Śakas."

The historical significance of this brief document is explained as follows by Bühler :—

"Some interesting historical information may be extracted from No. XXXIII, which records a gift by Kośikî Śi[va]mitrâ, [the wife] of Gotiputra, a black serpent for the Poṭhayas and Śakas.

Both Gotiputra and Kośikî Śivamitrâ were of noble or royal descent. This is indicated by their family names. *Kośiki*, in Sanskrit *Kauśikî*, means 'she of the race of Kuśika' Kauśika is the *nomen gentile* of Viśvamitra and his descendants, the Viśvâmitras, who form one of the ancient Vedic *gotras*. Numerous instances in the northern and southern inscription show that the queens and princesses were frequently called by the Vedic *gotra*-names, such as the Gautamî, the Vâtsî, the Vâsishṭhî, the Gârgî, etc. And the explanation is no doubt that these *gotras* originally were those of the Purohitas of the royal or noble families, from which the queens were descended, and that the kings were affiliated to them for religious reasons as the *Śrautasûtras* indicate. It seems, therefore, impossible to explain the epithet Kośikî otherwise than by the assumption that Śivamitrâ was descended from a royal race, which had been affiliated to the Kauśikas.

With respect to Gotiputra, in Sanskrit Gauptîputra, it may be pointed out that this name, which means the son of her of the Gaupta race, is borne by the second king of Sir A. Cunningham's inscription on the *Toraṇa* of the Bharhut *Stûpa*, where we read *Gotiputrasa Âgarajusa puteṇa*, in Sanskrit *Gauptîputrasya Aṅgâradyutaḥ putreṇa*. Though I am not prepared to identify the two Gotiputras, it is evident that the name was borne at least by one royal or princely personage. The epithet of our Gotiputra, 'a black serpent for the Poṭhayas and Śakas,' points also to his belonging to the warrior tribe. For, according to the analogy of other well-known epithets, such as *vairimattebhasiṁha*, it can only mean that he fought with the Poṭhayas and Śakas, and proved to them as destructive as the black cobra is to mankind in general.

The Poṭhayas are the Proshṭhas, whom the *Mahâbhârata*, Volume VI, pages 9, 61, and the *Vishṇupurâṇa* (ed. Hall, Volume II, page 179), name among the southern nations. In the latter passage they appear together with the Śakas and the Kokarakas. As both works include in their enumeration of the southern nations the Trigartas, who are known to be inhabitants of Northern India, the accuracy of their statements with respect to the seats of the Śakas and Proshṭhas may be doubted. But it remains interesting that the two names are placed closely together in the *Vishṇupurâṇa*, and this juxtaposition is, as our inscription shows, not without foundation."[1]

The characters of the inscription being archaic, the wars alluded to probably took place in the first century B. C. The Śakas may have been the Satraps (*Kshatrapa*) of Mathurâ.

Figure 2 of the plate represents a pretty bit of scroll work, well undercut.

[1] Bühler in "Epigraphia Indica," Vol. I, pp. 394, 396, Inscr. No. XXXIII. Bühler's explanation of the formation of the names of queens and princesses is not universally accepted.

Fig. 2. Fragment of Carved Panel.

Fig. 1. Fragment of Âyâgapaṭa, or "Tablet of Homage," set up by Śivamitrâ, the Wife of Gotiputra.

Scale of Feet

Inches 12 9 6 3 0 1 Foot

MATHURÂ SERIES.—KANKÂLÎ TÎLÂ.

IMAGE OF ÂRYAVATÎ, SET UP FOR THE WORSHIP OF THE ARHATS BY AMOHINÎ, THE WIFE OF PÂLA, IN THE 42ND YEAR OF THE MAHÂKSHATRAPA SODÂSA.

SCALE OF FEET

INCHES 12 9 6 3 0 1 FOOT

PLATE XIV.

IMAGE OF ÂRYAVATÎ, DATED IN THE 42ND YEAR OF THE SATRAP SODÂSA.

THIS fine votive tablet, which is essentially an *âyâgapaṭa*, though not so called, represents a royal lady attended by three women and a child. The attendant women, in accordance with the ancient Hindu fashion, which survived to modern times in Southern India, are naked to the waist. One holds an umbrella over her mistress, whom another fans. The third holds a wreath *(hâr)* ready for presentation. The execution is bold, and not altogether wanting in artistic merit.

The inscription above shows that the tablet was presented to the Jain shrine by a lady named Amohinî in the year 42, in the reign of the Satrap Śodâsa. The text is as follows :—

L.1. *Nama arahato Vardhamânasa*

2. *Sv[á]misa mahakshatrapasa Śoḍâsasa savatsare XL (?) II hemaṅtamâse II divase IX Haritiputrasa Pâlasa bhayâye samasârikâye*

3. *Kochhiye Amohiniye sahâ putrehi Pâlaghoshena Poṭhaghoshena Dhanaghoshena Âyavati pratithâpitâ prâya[bha]*

4. *Âryavati arahatapujâye.*

The record, which presents many points of interest, is rendered as follows by Bühler :—

"Adoration to the Arhat Vardhamâna! In the year 42 of the Lord, the Mahâkshatrapa Śoḍâsa, in the second month of winter, on the 9th day, an Âyavatî *(Âryavatî)* was set up by Amohini *(Amohinî)*, the Kochhi *(Kautsî)*, a female lay-disciple of the ascetics *(and)* wife of Pâla, son of a Hariti *(Haritî or Hâritî mother)*, together with her sons Pâlaghosha, Poṭhaghosha *(Proshṭhaghosha, and)* Dhanaghosha . . . . the Âryavatî *(is)* for the worship of the Arhat."[1]

Unfortunately the initial year of the era used by the great Satrap Śoḍâsa has not yet been determined with accuracy, but the inscription may be considered as dating a few years earlier than the Christian era. Although Bühler thought it possible that the first numeral character might be read as 70, it seems to me to be 40.

Another inscription of the Satrap Śoḍâsa was found by Cunningham in the Jail mound at Mathurâ (*Arch. Rep.*, Volume III, page 30, Plate XIII, 1). His coins also are found in the neighbourhood. His history and coinage are discussed in the publications referred to in the note,[2] but no thoroughly satisfactory result can be obtained until the chronological position of the dynasty of the Satraps of Mathurâ is definitely fixed

[1] "Epigraphia Indica," Vol. II, p. 199, Inscr. No. II. M. Boyer (*L'Époque de Kaṇiska*, p. 566) accepts 72 as correct.

[2] Cunningham, "Coins of Ancient India," p. 86, Plate VIII; Bhagwân Lâl Indraji and Rapson in J. R. A. S. for 1894, pp. 541 *seqq.* Bühler, *ibidem*, pp. 525 *seqq.*

CHAPTER IV.—VENERATION OF A STUPA.

PLATE XV.

VENERATION OF A *STŪPA*.

This plate represents the carvings on the obverse, reverse, and under-side, or soffit, of the central portion of the lowest beam of a *Toraṇa* archway in the railing round a *Stūpa*.[1] The beam was found in January 1891 north of the well and near one of the Jain temples. It may have belonged to the ancient *Stūpa*, which was believed to have been built by the gods (*ante*, Plate VI), and is certainly an early work, probably to be dated about 100 or 50 B. C.

The scenes on the obverse and reverse have already been reproduced by Bühler from photographs.[2] The *patera* on the under-side is now published for the first time.

Bühler's description is as follows :—

"The obverse represents the worship[3] of a *Stūpa* by two Suparṇas, half birds and half men, and by five centaurs or Kiṁnaras. One of the former offers a garland and the other, as well as three of the centaurs, two on the right and one on the left, bring jars or boxes fitted with flower bunches(?). The last two centaurs on the left seem to carry brooms or fans, made of branches.[4] On both sides of the *Stūpa* stand trees, and the two Suparṇas seem to be seated on, or hovering above, the bending branches of those nearest to the *Stūpa*. All the five figures wear turbans, such as many of the males of rank represented on Buddhist sculptures wear

A somewhat similar scene, where Suparṇas worship a *Stūpa*, occurs on a relievo at Sanchi. (Fergusson, *Tree and Serpent Worship*, Plate XXVIII, figure 1.) But it must be noted that the Sanchi figures are much more like Greek harpies, while those on our slab are done in a more conventional manner like the winged figures on the Assyrian and Persian sculptures.

Among Brahmanical representations, those of Garuḍa, the king of the Suparṇas, on the Gupta seals are worthy of comparison. Centaurs have been discovered on the Buddhist monuments in Gayâ and elsewhere, and in all probability, they go back to Greek models. What is particularly remarkable in those on our slab is the branch which hides the place where the human body is united with the rump of the horse. As far as I have been able to ascertain from my colleagues, versed in classical archæology, there are no Greek sculptures showing this particular.

The reverse of our doorstep [*sic*] contains a fragment of a procession, apparently about to visit some sacred place. On the extreme right we have two horsemen, each preceded by a '*syce*' or groom. Next follows a covered cart, drawn by two enormous bullocks, as big as those of the Pâlanpur breed, and filled with males and females. The cart closely resembles a modern shighram, and the driver, who lifts his goad, is seated, as is still the custom, on the pole. The tails of the animals are tied to strings connected with the yoke, just as is the case with those of the horses on the Sanchi relievos. Behind the cart comes again a horseman and finally an elephant with two riders. The elephant is very badly done.[5] The trappings of the several animals are exactly like those represented on the Sanchi sculptures. But similar carts are not traceable on the latter, where very Greek-looking chariots drawn by horses appear instead.

---

[1] Bühler erroneously calls the beam a doorstep. The under-surface of a doorstep would not be carved.

[2] "Epigraphia Indica," Vol. II, p. 318, Plate II, figs. *b* and *c*.

[3] I prefer to use the word "veneration" rather than "worship," which latter word as used in modern English is apt to cause misconception.

[4] I cannot discern any traces of bunches of flowers in the flat bowls. The objects described as brooms by Bühler are more correctly described by Mr. Mukherji, who notes that the fourth Kiṁnara holds a fly-flapper, and the fifth a lotus.

[5] This opinion seems to be due to imperfection in the photograph. The drawing now published shows that the elephant is represented with considerable skill. It is well-known that Indian sculptors and painters are more successful in representing the elephant than they are in representing any other animal.

MATHURA SERIES.—KANKÂLÎ TÎLÂ.

Reverse of Torana Beam representing a Procession about to visit some sacred place.

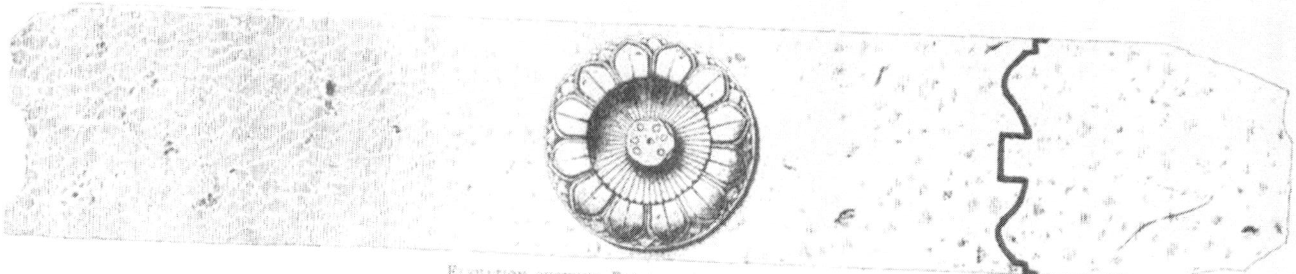

Elevation showing Patera beneath the Torana.

Obverse of Torana Beam representing the Worship of a Stûpa by two Suparnas, or Harpies, and five Kinnaras, or Centaurs.

Inches 12 9 6 3 Scale of Feet 1 Foot

Photo-lithographed at the Survey of India Offices, Calcutta, October [illegible]

FRAGMENTS OF SLABS REPRESENTING SUPARNAS, OR HARPIES.

Fig. 1.

Fig. 2.

SCALE OF FEET

INCHES 12 9 6 3 · 1 FOOT

PLATE XVI.

GANDHARVA AND SUPARṆAS.

THE figures in this plate may be regarded as a supplement to, and illustration of, the plate last described. The two fragments, as Mr. Mukherji points out, seem to be parts of one slab, which doubtless exhibited the veneration of a *Stûpa* by the heavenly beings. The left side of figure 2 should apparently be fitted to the top of figure 1. The mutilated male figure to the left of the umbrella seems to be intended for a *Gandharva*. A corresponding figure must have been on the other side of the umbrella. The *Kiṁnaras*, or harpies, hover in the air on each side of the umbrella over the lost *Stûpa*. The sculpture is archaic in style.

The "Tîrthakalpa" gives a description of the homage paid to "the *Stûpa* built by the gods" (*ante*, Plate VI), which illustrates Plates XV and XVI :—

"Then on the night of the eleventh [*scil* of the month Kârttika, October-November], holding vessels in their hands, they washed (the *Stûpa*) with milk, sour-milk, *ghi*, saffron, sandal, and so forth, out of thousands of vessels. The gods, remaining hidden, took part in the ablutions. Even to-day they come in the same way to the procession. When all by turns had performed the ablutions, they placed (on the *Stûpa*) flowers, incense, cloth, great banners, and ornaments. To the saints they gave clothes, *ghi*, sugar, and so forth. On the twelfth (night) garlands were put up."[1]

[1] Bühler, "A Legend of the Jaina *Stûpa* at Mathurâ." ("*Sitzungsberichte der Kais, Akad. der Wissensch. in Wien*," 1897.)

CHAPTER V.—SCULPTURED PANELS.

PLATE XVII.

SCULPTURED PANELS.

The broken slabs represented in this plate may have formed part of the decoration of a *Toraṇa* pillar.

Figure 1 represents a Jain saint, called Vardhamâna by Dr. Führer,[1] preaching to a prince and his three attendants. The royal rank of the principal hearer is indicated by the umbrella held over him.[2] The scene is bounded on the left by a lion capital in Achæmenian style.

The panel represented in figure 2 is divided into two compartments. The upper compartment, a narrow band, shows a *Stûpa* in the centre, with two seated Jainas on each side. These four images are probably those of the last four Tîrthaṁkaras, Nimi, Nemi, Pârśva, and Vardhamâna. The identity of Pârśvanâth is established by his canopy of snake-heads.

The lower compartment seems to represent the ascetic named Kaṇha, in whose honour the sculpture was dedicated, receiving the homage of the donor, the wife of Dhanahastin, and of three small females, one of whom is represented as a snake-maiden (*Nâga-kanyâ*) with a canopy of cobras. The objects held in the hands of the ascetic seem to be pieces of cloth. The principal inscription is in rather irregular characters. The date at the beginning appears to be 95, which would fall in the reign of Vâsudeva. The record is imperfect, and is not included among the inscriptions published by Dr. Bühler in the "Epigraphia Indica."

So far as it can be made out it reads :—

L. 1. [*Si*]*ddhaṁ saṁ XCV* (*?*) *gri II di XVIII Koṭṭiy*[*â*]*to gaṇâto Thâniyâto kulâto Vaïr*[*âto*] [*śâ*]*khâto Aryya araha* . . .

L. 2. *Śiśini Dhâmathâye* (*?*) *Grahadatasya dhi* . . *Dhanahathi* . . .

"Success ! In the year 95 (?), in the second (month of) summer, on the 18th day, at the request of Dhâmathâ (?), the female pupil of the Aryya Araha[dinna], from the Koṭṭiya *gaṇa*, from the Thâniya *kula*, from the Vaïra *śâkha* . . . . [the gift] of . . . . the daughter of Grahadata, and wife of Dhanathi (Dhanahastin)."

The words *anagha śreshṭi vidyâ* in large bold characters are to the proper right of the lady's head, and the words *Kaṇha Srâmaṇo* between her head and that of the ascetic.[3]

The sculpture evidently refers to some Jain legend which has not yet come to the knowledge of European scholars. The fact that Kaṇha is represented as clothed indicates that he belonged to the Śvetâmbara sect.

---

[1] I cannot discover any reason for calling the saint Vardhamâna.

[2] The prince's headdress resembles that shown on some gold coins of Huvishka.

[3] The words *Kaṇha Srâmaṇo* are distinct on the plate, but of *anagha śreshṭi vidyâ* only a portion is legible and the reading is doubtful. The reading is given by Führer in the "Progress Report" for 1890-91, page 15.

Fig. 1. Sculptured Panel representing Vardhamâna preaching to Royalty.

Fig. 2. Sculptured Panel representing the Jaina ascetic Kanha, the gift of the wife of Dhanahastin, dated Samvat 95.

Scale of Feet

Inches 12 9 6 3 1 Foot

Photo-Lithographed at the Survey of India Offices, Calcutta

Obverse of Ornamental Slab representing Naigameshâ-Nemeso, who at Indra's command transferred the embryo of Mahâvîra from the body of the Brâhmanî Devanandâ to the womb of the Kshatriyânî Trisalâ.

Reverse of Ornamental Slab representing female Dancers and Musicians rejoicing at Nemesa's feat.

Scale of Feet

Inches 12 9 6 3 1 Foot

Photo-lithographed at the Survey of India Offices, Calcutta, October [illegible]

CHAPTER VI.—NAIGAMESHA NEMESA.

PLATE XVIII.

NAIGAMESHA NEMESA.

This plate represents the obverse and reverse of a broken frieze about two feet in length and is, perhaps, the most interesting of the series.

The extant portion of the obverse shows five figures. The principal figure is a goat-headed deity seated in an easy attitude on a low seat, turning round his head to the proper right as if addressing another personage whose image has been lost. The deity is labelled *Bhagavâ Nemeso* in bold characters, dating from about the beginning of the Christian era, or earlier. To the right are three standing females, and a male infant stands by the left knee of the deity. The reverse of the slab shows nine figures of musicians and dancers, of whom six are practically complete.

The late Dr. Bühler published a photograph of the obverse of the slab ("Epigraphia Indica," Volume II, page 314, Plate II[1]), and succeeded in clearly explaining the meaning of the group.

Bhagavâ Nemeso, 'the worshipful Nemeso,'[2] is a variant of the name of the deity called *Hariṇegamesī* in the *Kalpasûtra*, *Naigameshin* in the *Neminâtha charita*, and *Nejamesha* or *Naigameya* in other works. The god is represented sometimes with the head of a ram, sometimes with that of an antelope, and sometimes with that of a goat. In all his forms, whether in Jain or Brahmanical mythology, he is associated with the procreation of children. He is regarded in two aspects—one as a beneficent, and the other as a malevolent, deity.

Bühler relates the legend illustrated by the sculpture from the *Kalpasûtra* as follows :—

"When Indra became aware that Mahâvira had taken the form of an embryo in the Brâhmaṇī Devanandâ's body, he paid his reverence to the Arhat that was to be born. It then occurred to him that an Arhat ought not to be born in a low Brahmanical family, but only in a noble royal race, and that it was and always had been the duty of the reigning Indra to transfer the embryo, in case through the influence of his *Karman* an Arhat had descended into the body of a female of the Brahman caste. In order to fulfil this duty, Indra directed Hariṇegamesī, the divine commander of infantry, to transfer Mahâvira from the body of Devanandâ to Triśâlâ, a lady of the Jnâtṛi family of Kshatriyas, who was also with child. Hariṇagamesī then repaired first to the Brahmanical quarter of Kuṇḍagrâma,[3] took Mahâvira from Devanandâ, cleansing him from all impurity, and carried him carefully in his folded hands to the Kshatriya quarter of the same town. There he took Triśâlâ's embryo from her, likewise duly cleansing it, and put Mahâvira in its place. Next he returned to Devanandâ and placed Triśâlâ's child in her body. During these operations the two ladies and their attendants lay in a deep magic sleep. Finally, the deity returned to Indra's abode and reported to him that his orders had been carried out."

The missing personage addressed by the goat-headed god must have been Indra. The scene of the composition should, therefore, be regarded as laid in Indra's heaven after the execution of the mission. The infant seems to hold in his left hand a cloth, and to be thus conventionally indicated as an ascetic. He must be identified with Mahâvira. The imperfect legend *Bhaga*[*vâ*] seems from its position to refer to the central female, who is apparently intended for either Devanandâ or Triśâlâ; but the epithet, which means "worshipful," is more appropriate if referred to the infant Mahâvira.

[1] The inscription is separately published in *ibid*, p. 200, No. VI.

[2] Bühler translates *bhagavâ* by "divine," but "worshipful" is a safer rendering.

[3] Vaisâli, the modern Basârh, about 27 miles north of Patna, comprised three distinct sections, Vaisâli, Kundagâma, and Vaniyagâma, the modern villages of Basârh (बसाढ), Basukund, and Baniyâ. The suburb Kollâga was occupied by the Kshatriya clan of the Nâtas or Nâyas, whose chief was Siddhârtha, the father of Vardhamâna or Mahâvira, the founder of Jainism. The birth of Mahâvira took place in or about B. C. 599, all, or nearly all, authorities are agreed that he died in B. C. 527. (Hoernle, "Annual Address to Asiatic Society of Bengal," February 1898, in *Proc. A. S. B.* for that month.)

The group on the reverse of the slab is evidently designed as an expression of rejoicing at the successful accomplishment of the transfer of the child.

The contemptuous reference in the *Kalpasûtra* to "a low Brahmanical family" is of interest.

Bühler points out that four mutilated statues, or statuettes, now in the Mathurâ Museum, which puzzled Cunningham, refer to the same legend. Two of these figures are goat-headed males and two are females, each holding an infant in a dish.[1]

---

[1] Cunningham, "Reports," Vol. XX, p. 36, Plate IV. The heads are mutilated and Cunningham supposed the figures to be "ox-headed;" but they are either "goat-headed" or "ram-headed." No record has been kept of the locality in which these curious figures were found.

PLATE XX.

MATHURA SERIES.—KANKÂLÎ TÎLÂ.

Reverse of Torana, representing gods and men paying homage to the Stûpas and Temples of the Tîrthamkaras.

Scale of Feet

Inches 12 9 6 3 0 1 Foot

Photo-zincographed at the Survey of India Offices, Calcutta, October 1896.

MATHURA SERIES.—KANKÂLÎ TÎLÂ.

OBVERSE OF TORANA, REPRESENTING GODS AND MEN PAYING HOMAGE TO THE TÎRTHAMKARAS.

SCALE OF FEET

INCHES 12 9 6 3 0 1 FOOT

Photo-zincographed at the Survey of India Offices, Calcutta, [illegible]

CHAPTER VII.—A TORANA.

PLATES XIX AND XX.

A *TORAṆA*.

THE interesting sculptures which are the subject of these plates formed part of the decoration of the obverse and reverse of a *Toraṇa* archway, such as is represented in plate XII *ante*. They have already been reproduced from photographs and described by Bühler (*Epigraphia Indica*, Volume II, p. 319, Plate III).

The general subject of both compositions is the veneration of holy objects and places, probably Jain, by human and mythological beings. The plates are so readily intelligible that detailed description may be spared, and the reader's attention need be merely drawn to a few noticeable points.

The spandril, or corner space, in Plate XIX represents a group of ten male and female worshippers standing in an attitude of adoration, and bringing offerings. Below their feet a cart is shown in part. The central and most conspicuous figure carries a large wreath to be hung up on the *Stûpa* or temple. The three curved bands all represent processional scenes, and may be compared with Plate XV *ante*. The running figures in the central band carry long trailing wreaths. This motive is very common in Indian Buddhist art and in Roman art of the Antonine period, and as late as the time of Constantine (A. D. 300). The style of this central band seems to me decidedly Hellenistic. The open-mouthed crocodiles which terminate each band are a very common element of decoration in early Indian art.

On the reverse (Plate XX) the spandril is again occupied by a group of worshippers, six in number, engaged in doing reverence to a *Stûpa* and three small platforms bearing representations of sacred emblems.[1] The processional scenes in the carved bands are largely occupied by mythical monsters.

There is nothing in the sculptures of this *Toraṇa* to indicate whether the ceremony depicted was Jain or Buddhist; but the fact that the slabs were found not far from the present temple of Kankâlî and close to many Jain remains indicates that Jain ceremonies are the subject of the composition.

Bühler has correctly pointed out that there was no distinctive school of Buddhist, as distinguished from Jain and Brahmanical, art. All sects made use for devotional purposes of the art style of their period, and all alike to a very large extent used the same symbolism. Wheels, tridents, lotus flowers, *Stûpas*, and many other forms of symbols are common to all the sects.

---

[1] Such platforms were called *pîṭhikâ*.

CHAPTER VIII.—DECORATIVE WORK.

PLATES XXI TO XXVI.

DECORATIVE WORK.

These six plates, which represent sundry specimens of uninscribed decorative work, may be grouped together, and very briefly described.

The panel shown in Plate XXI is a very fine example of deeply undercut scroll work, based on an acanthus leaf motive. It has been published as figure 3 of Plate VI of the "Technical Art Series," 1892.

Plate XXII represents another panel of a more commonplace kind, carved in shallow relief.[1] Such panels were used to cover blank spaces.[2] Plate XXIII represents a singularly perfect and delicately carved umbrella in red sandstone, which was probably suspended over a colossal statue, or perhaps over a *Stûpa*.[3]

The fragment of a *Toraṇa* beam depicted in figure 1 of Plate XXIV is exquisitely carved. The lotus flower and buds are admirably executed.[4] The squatted dwarf with snake extremities recalls a class of figures common in Græco-Roman art, and probably of Alexandrine origin.

Figure 2, a string course, is a good example of undercut leaf scroll work.

Plate XXV offers examples of the carved ends of *Toraṇa* beams.

The most interesting of these is shown in figure 1, which represents in the left compartment a bird monster, or *garuḍa*, in the act of devouring a triple-hooded snake, which has coiled itself round the monster's neck. The right compartment is unfortunately imperfect. The object depicted is a covered carriage with the bullocks unyoked and resting. One of the animals is standing, while the other is comfortably lying down. The perspective is unusually good.

The carved door jamb represented in Plate XXVI is said to have been found in the ruins at Moramayî, a village about seven miles west of Mathurâ, where an inscription of the Satrap Rajubula was discovered. The well-executed vine on the front elevation is noticeable, and is, I think, distinctly Hellenistic.

Plates XXIV, XXV, and XXVI have already been published as Plates 85 and 87 of the "Journal of Indian Art and Industry," Volume V, No. 44 (October 1893).

---

[1] This slab is said to have been found in the so-called Jail mound Cunningham's name of "the Jail mound" refers to the old and disused Jail.

[2] Compare the similar decorative panels between the *Toraṇa* beams in Plate XII *ante*.

[3] This specimen is also said to come from the Jail mound. Two inferior umbrellas, now in the Lucknow Museum, wereo fund in the Kankâli mound in February 1889.

[4] The lotus was the symbol of the 6th Jina, Supadmanâtha. I need hardly say that the lotus is used in Indian art of all ages and all religions.

MATHURA SERIES.—KANKÂLÎ TÎLÂ. PLATE XXI.

DETAILS OF CARVED PANEL.

SCALE OF FEET

INCHES 12 9 6 3 0 1 FOOT

MATHURA SERIES.—KANKÂLÎ TÎLÂ.

DETAILS OF CARVED PANEL.

SCALE OF FEET

INCHES 12 9 6 3 ∴ 1 2 FEET

Photo-zincographed at the Survey of India Offices, Calcutta, October [illegible]

RED SANDSTONE UMBRELLA.

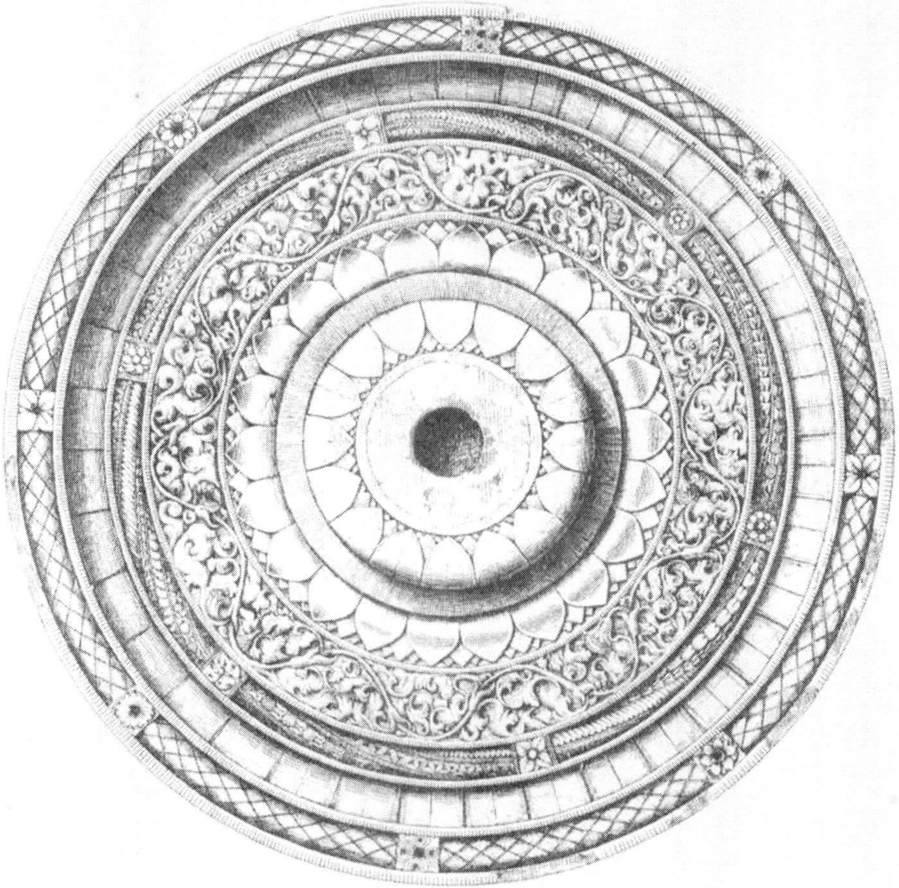

CARVED UNDER SURFACE.

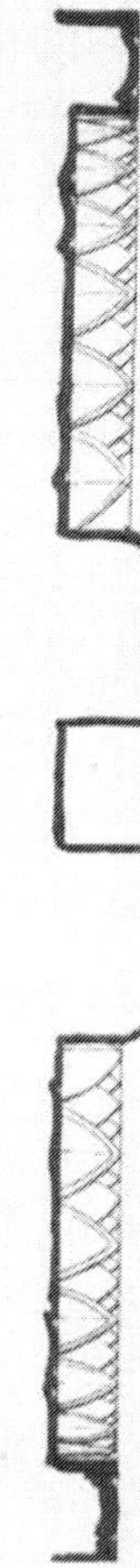

SECTION.

SCALE OF FEET

INCHES 12 9 6 3 0 1 2 3 FEET

Photo-zincographed at the Survey of India Offices, Calcutta, October [illegible]

MATHURA SERIES.—KANKÂLÎ TÎLÂ.

Fig. 1. Details of Carved Torana Beam.

Fig. 2. Details of Carved String-course.

Scale of Feet

Inches 12 9 6 3 1 2 3 Feet

Photo-lithographed at the Survey of India Offices, Calcutta, October [illegible]

MATHURA SERIES.—KANKALI TILA.

PLATE XXV

Ends of Toran Beams.

Fig. 1. Front Elevation.

Side Elevation.

Fig. 2. Back Elevation.

Section.

Front Elevation.

Scale of Feet

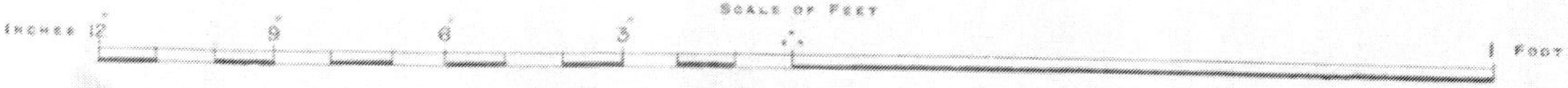

Photo-zincographed at the Survey of India Offices, Calcutta, October [illegible].

MATHURA SERIES.—KANKÂLÎ TÎLÂ.

Carved Door-jamb.

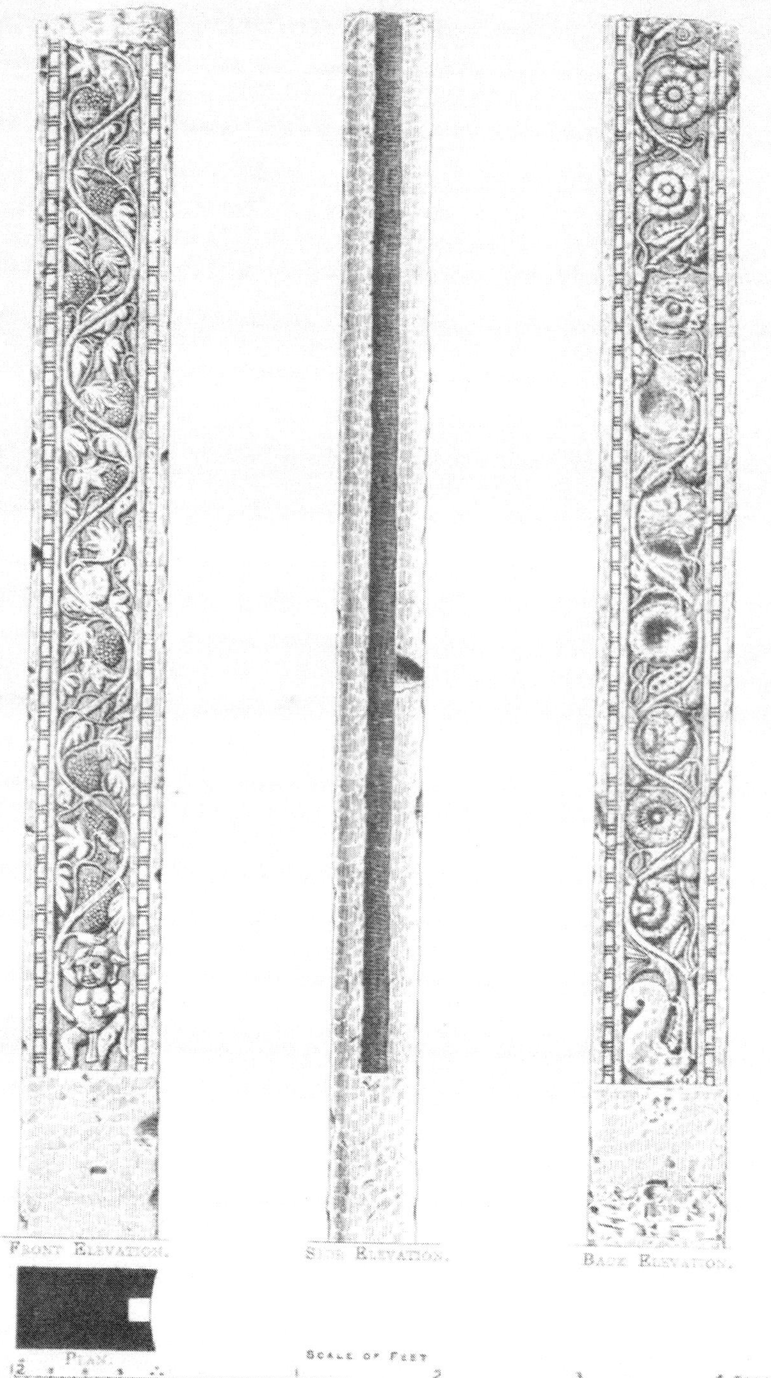

Photo-zincographed at the Survey of India Offices, Calcutta, October [illegible]

MATHURA SERIES.—KANKÂLÎ TÎLÂ.

FRAGMENT OF TORANA PILLAR ERECTED BY BALAHASTINÂ. PLATE XXVIII.

FRONT ELEVATION.

BACK ELEVATION.

PLAN.

Chromo-lithographed at the Survey of India Offices, Calcutta, October 18[illegible]

SIDE ELEVATION. BACK ELEVATION. FRONT ELEVATION.

SCULPTURED PILLAR OF TORANA.

INCHES 12 9 6 3 SCALE OF FEET 1 2 FEET

Photo-zincographed at the Survey of India Offices, Calcutta, October [illegible]

CHAPTER IX.—TORANA PILLARS.

PLATES XXVII AND XXVIII.

TORAṆA PILLARS.

EACH pillar is divided into a series of compartments, one above the other, and each compartment contains the representation of a domestic scene. The compartments are separated by railings with plain bars and posts. The arrangement of the compartments resembles that seen in the Gândhâra sculptures; but the debased Corinthian capitals characteristic of those sculptures are here wanting. Plate XXVII has been already published as Plate 86 of No. 44 of Volume V of the "Journal of Indian Art and Industry" for October 1893.

The attitude of the figures in the upper compartment of the back elevation of the inscribed pillar shown in Plate XXVIII is indelicate. The principal figure in the lower compartment of the same pillar is evidently intended for a king or chief. The inscription, which is in characters dating apparently from the time of the great Kushân kings, reads as follows :—

L. 1. "*Namâ ahaṁtânaṁ* [*sic*] *śrâmaṇa śrarikâye.*
2. *lahastiniye toranaṁ prati*[*shṭhâpi*].
3. *saha mâtâ pitihi saha.*
4. *saśrû śaśureṇa.*

"Adoration to the Arhats! A *Toraṇa* has been erected by order of—lahastini (*Balahastinî*), a lay pupil of the ascetics, together with her parents, together with her mother-in-law and her father-in-law."[1]

The formula was intended to secure the participation of the relatives named in the merit of the young lady's pious act.

The Mathurâ inscriptions afford many clear proofs that the ladies formed an influential element in the constitution of the early Jain church.

[1] "Epigraphia Indica," Vol. I, p. 390, No. XVII.

CHAPTER X.—SUNDRY CARVINGS.

PLATES XXIX, XXX, AND XXXI.

SUNDRY CARVINGS.

FIGURE 1 in Plate XXIX, unfortunately much mutilated, represents a horseman riding up a rocky ascent. The principal element in figures 2 and 3 of the same plate may be regarded as a variety of the *vajra*, or thunderbolt, commonly used in the later Buddhist symbolism.

Plate XXX represents a well-preserved and beautifully-carved lintel. Part of another lintel with lions' or tigers' heads on the dentils is shown in figure 2 of Plate XXXI. The pediment shown in figure 1 of that plate must have formed part of the decoration of a temple steeple. It is said to come from the Kesava temple in the city of Mathurâ, and not from the Kankâli mound.

The seated deity with a lotus in each hand appears to be intended for the Sun-god.

MATHURA SERIES.—KANKĀLĪ ṬĪLĀ.

Decorative Ornaments.

Fig. 1.

Front Elevation.

Fig. 2.

Side Elevation.

Back Elevation.

Fig. 3.

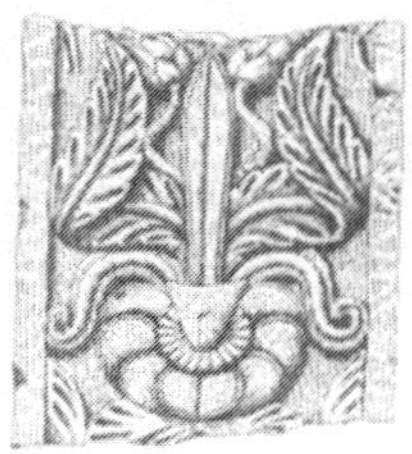

Fig. 4.

Front Elevation.

Fig. 5.

Back Elevation.

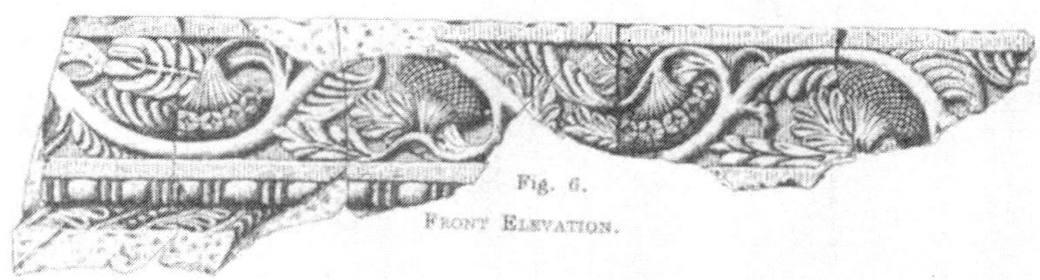

Fig. 6.

Front Elevation.

Section.

Scale of Feet

Inches 12 9 6 3 0 1 Foot

Khoda Mul

Photo-zincographed at the Survey of India Offices, Calcutta, October 1898.

MATHURA SERIES.—KANKÂLÎ TÎLÂ.

CARVED DOOR LINTEL.

SCALE OF FEET.

INCHES 12 9 6 3 · 1 FOOT

Photo-zincographed at the Survey of India Offices, Calcutta, October [illegible]

MATHURÂ SERIES.—KANKÂLÎ TÎLÂ

Fig. 1. Details of Carved Pediment.

Section.

Front Elevation

Fig. 2. Fragment of Carved Door Lintel.

Scale of Feet

Inches 12" 9 6 3 0 1 Foot

MATHURA SERIES.—KANKÂLÎ TÎLÂ.

FRAGMENT OF SCULPTURED TORANA.

PLATE XXXIII.

BACK ELEVATION

Fig. 1.

FRONT ELEVATION.

Fig. 2.

INCHES 12" 9" 6" 3" SCALE OF FEET 1 FOOT

MATHURA SERIES.—KANKÂLÎ TÎLÂ.

FRAGMENT OF SCULPTURED TORANA.

FRONT ELEVATION.

SIDE ELEVATION.

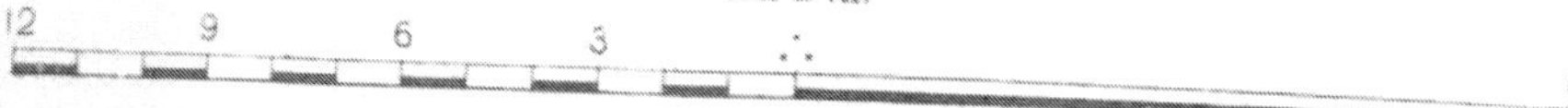

Photozincographed at the Survey of India Offices, Calcutta, October

PLATES XXXII AND XXXIII.

FIGURE SCULPTURES OF A *TORAṆA*.

THE sculptures shown in these plates formed part of the decorations of the jambs of a *toraṇa* gateway.

The persons represented in the upper panel of figure 1 of Plate XXXII seem to be man and wife. Both are naked to the waist, except for a folded *dopatta* thrown over the shoulders.

The lower panel of the same figure offers a very curious picture of a woman playing cymbals, with her elbows resting on the sill of a window with a pointed arch. Below the window is a water-vessel (*lota*) with five lotus-buds in it. The object to the left is perhaps a bird.

Figure 1 in Plate XXXIII presents processional scenes on the back and front of the jamb. Women, naked to the waist, are bringing offerings to a holy place.

The group depicted in figure 2 of the same plate is unfortunately mutilated. The principal figure is a man of foreign appearance, squatted on the ground, playing a lute *(vīṇā)*. He is attended by two women, of whom one holds up a water-jar in her left hand, while the other holds a palm-leaf fan.

The man wears nothing but a tight waistcloth *(dhotī)*, a circular turban, and bracelets. The women wear heavy and numerous armlets.

PLATES XXXIV AND XXXV.

SCULPTURED BRACKETS OF *TORAṆA* BEAM.[1]

The principal figures appear to be those of dancing-girls, each standing under a tree.

In Plate XXXIV the girl is represented standing on an elephant with uplifted trunk. In Plate XXXV she stands upon the back of a nude female.

Both the girls are clothed below the waist and are not entirely nude like the women in Plates LX to LXIII *post*. The heavy anklets resemble those now worn in Bundelkhand.

[1] The bracket illustrated in plate C should have been described here.

PLATE XXXIV.

MATHURA SERIES.—KANKÂLÎ TÎLÂ.

SCULPTURED BRACKET, SUPPORTING VOLUTED END OF TORANA BEAM.

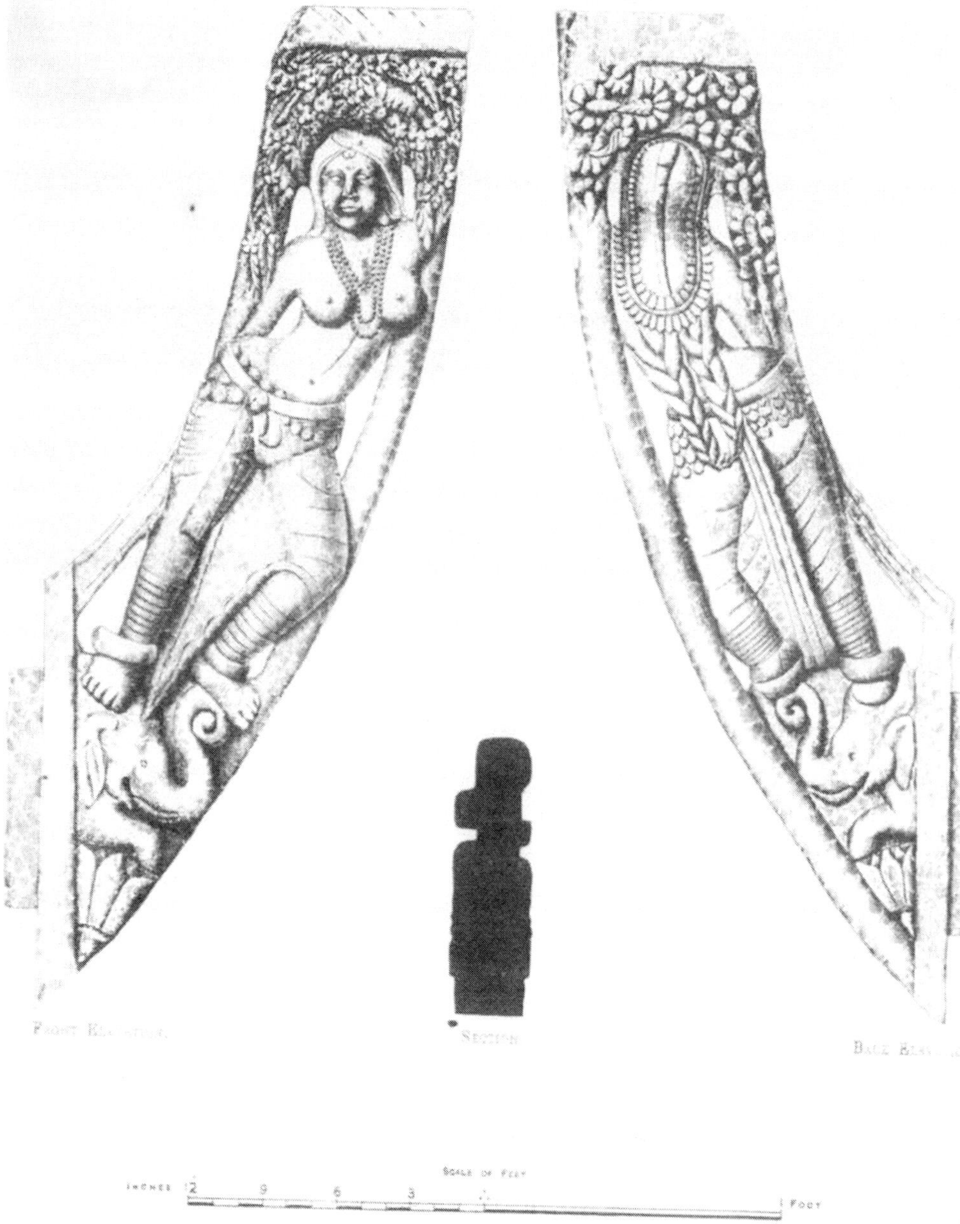

MATHURA SERIES.—KANKÂLÎ TÎLÂ.

Sculptured Bracket supporting voluted end of Torana Beam.

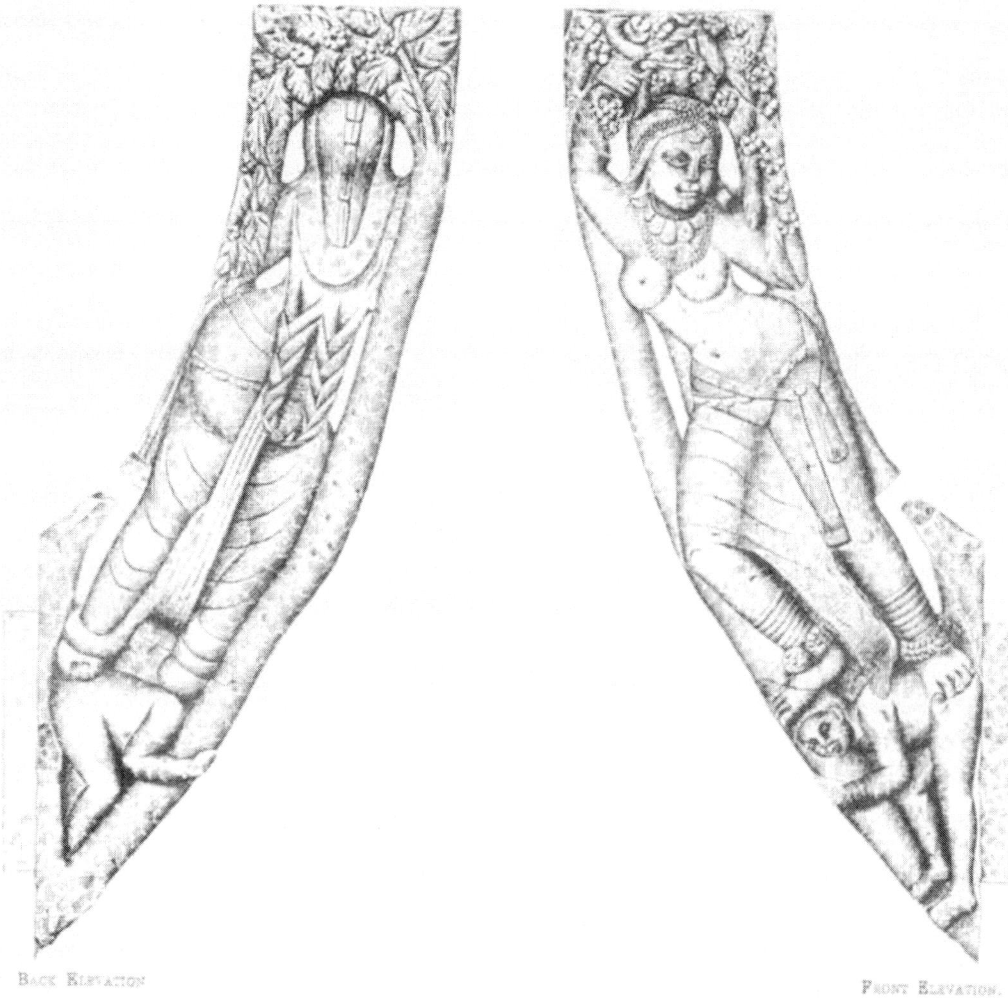

Back Elevation

Front Elevation.

Scale of Feet

Inches 12 9 6 3 0 1 Foot

MATHURA SERIES.—KANKÀLÌ TÎLÀ.

SCULPTURED BRACKETS.

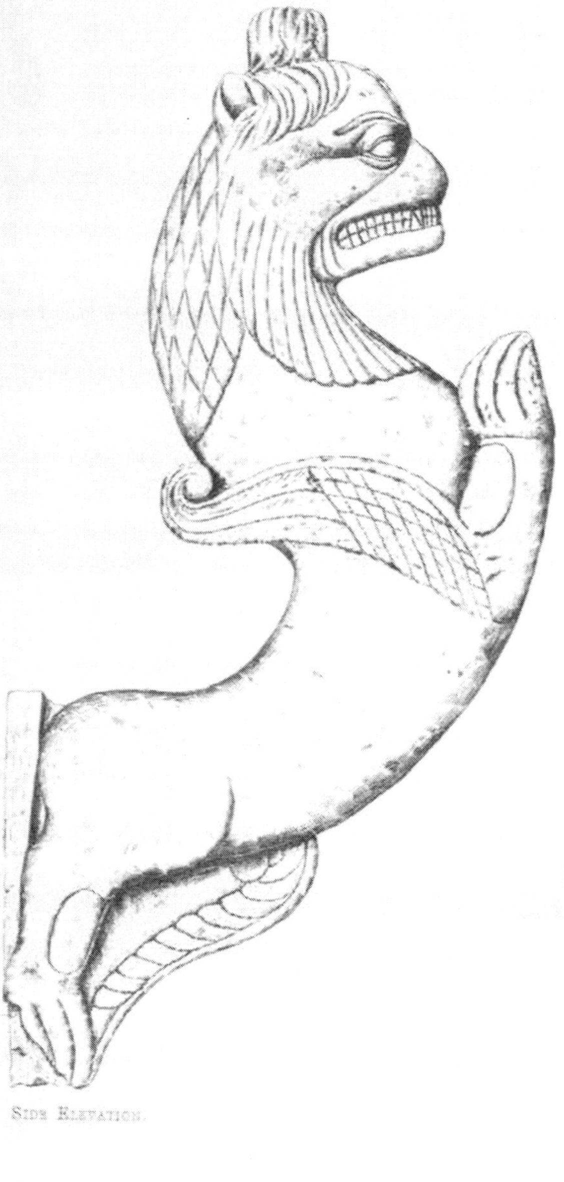

SIDE ELEVATION.

Fig. 1.

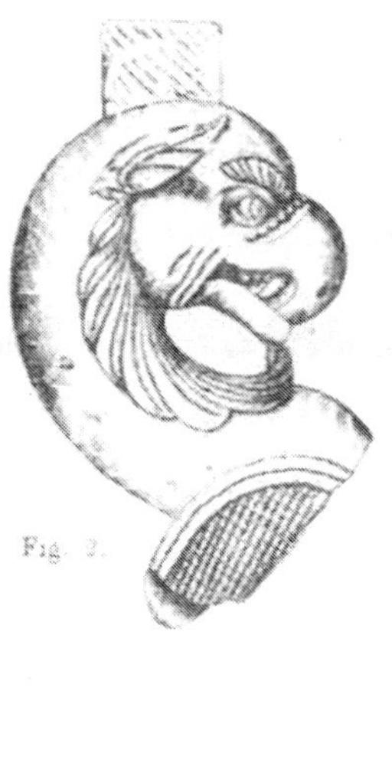

Fig. 2.

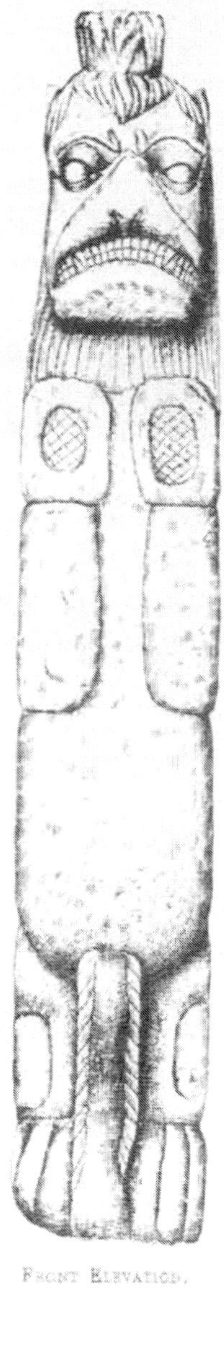

FRONT ELEVATION.

SCALE OF FEET

INCHES 12" 9 6 3 0 1 FOOT

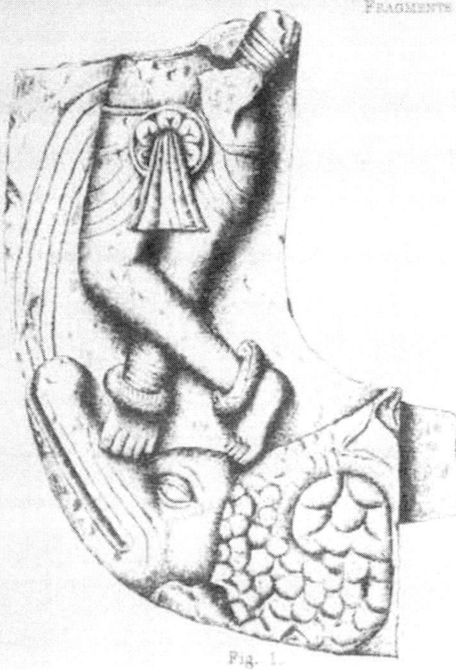

Fig. 1.

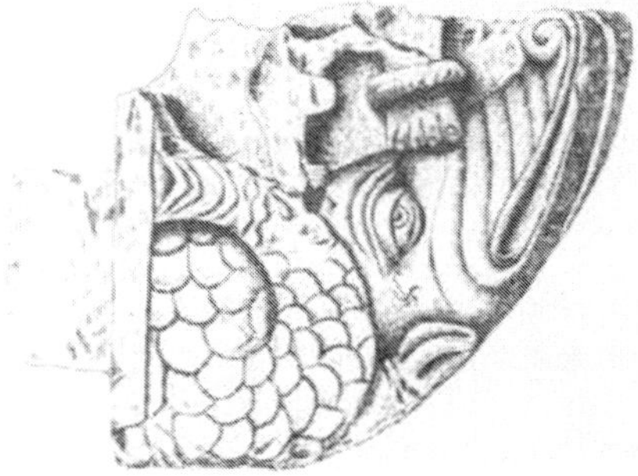

Fig. 2.

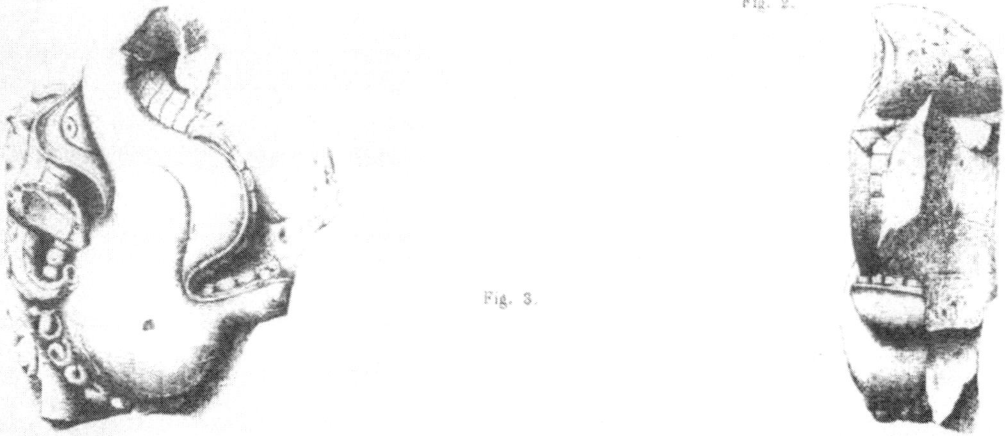

FRONT ELEVATION. Fig. 3. SIDE ELEVATION.

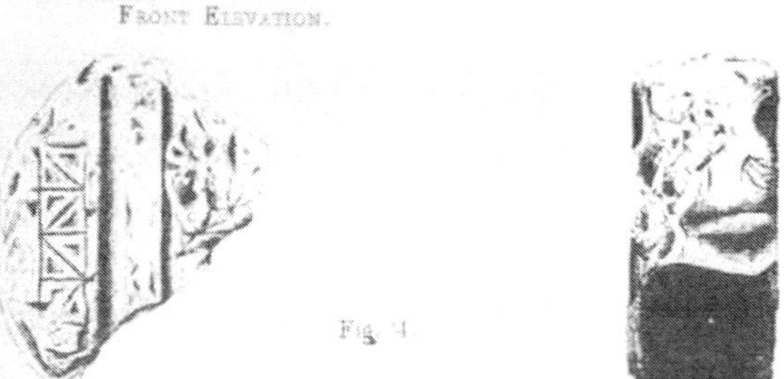

FRONT ELEVATION. Fig. 4 SIDE ELEVATION.

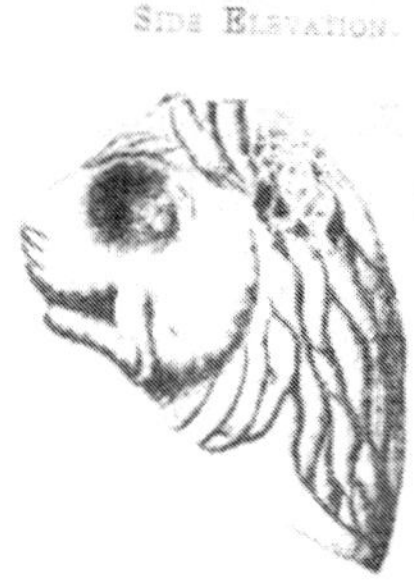

Fig. 5.

SCALE OF FEET

INCHES 12 9 6 3 0 1 FOOT

Photo-zincographed at the Survey of India Offices, Calcutta, October 18[illegible]

PLATES XXXVI AND XXXVII.

SCULPTURED BRACKETS.

The fragments illustrated in Plate **XXXVI** are too much mutilated to be of interest. Figure 1 in Plate **XXXVII** is that of a purely conventional winged lion with an Assyrian look.

PLATE XXXVIII.

BASES OF SMALL PILLARS.

These carvings are well executed. The principal motives employed are winged dragons, the *svastika*, or mystic cross, the honeysuckle, and the *vajra*, or thunderbolt. The *svastika* is the emblem of the seventh Jina, Supârśvanâth. The *vajra*, or thunderbolt, is the emblem of Dharmanâth, the fifteenth Jina.

CARVED BASES OF SMALL SQUARE PILLARS.

Fig. 1.

FRONT ELEVATION.

SIDE ELEVATION.

Fig. 2.

Fig. 3.

FRONT ELEVATION.

BACK ELEVATION.

Fig. 4.

SCALE OF FEET

INCHES 12 9 6 3 1 FOOT

Photo-zincographed at the Survey of India Offices, Calcutta

MATHURA SERIES.—KANKÂLÎ TÎLÂ.

SCULPTURED WATER-COURSES.

Fig. 1.

Fig. 3.

Fig. 2.

FRONT ELEVATION.

SECTION.

SCALE OF FEET

INCHES 12 9 6 3 0 1 2 FEET

MATHURA SERIES.—KANKÂLÎ TÎLÂ.

Perforated Windows.

Front Elevation. Fig. 1. Section.

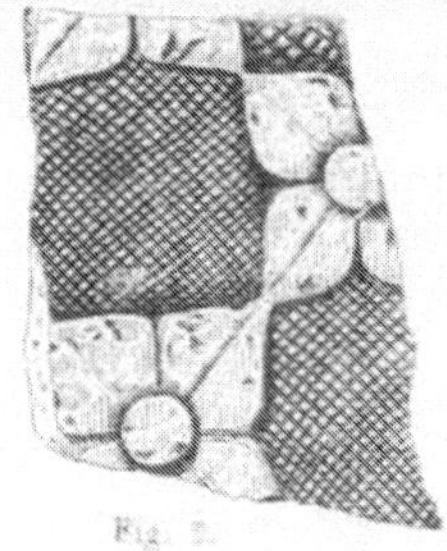

Fig. 2.

Scale of Feet

Inches 12 9 6 3 1 2 Feet

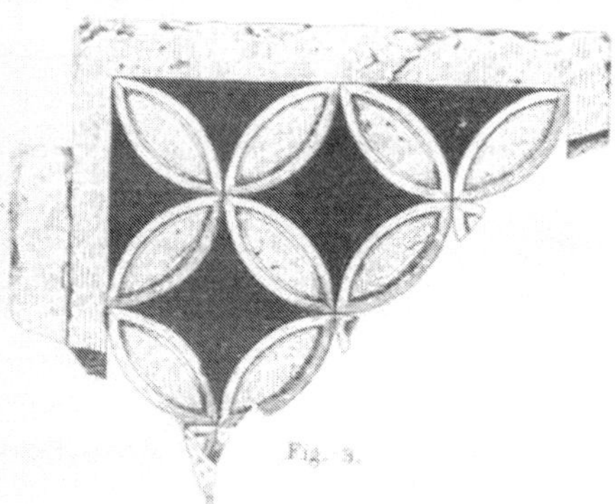

Fig. 3.

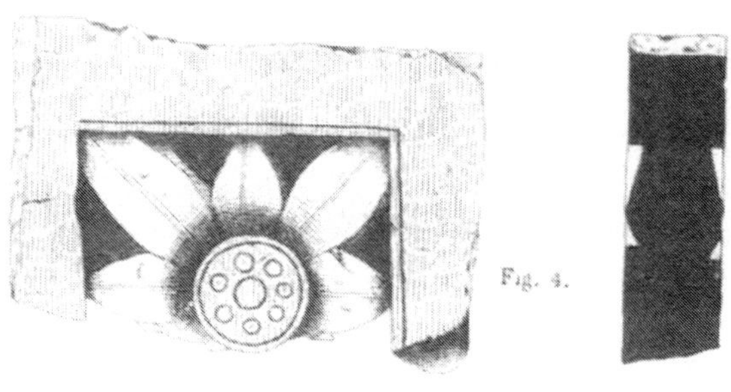

Front Elevation. Fig. 4. Section.

Scale of Feet

Inches 12 9 6 3 1 Foot

MATHURA SERIES.—KANKÂLÎ TÎLÂ.

Carved Pinnacle of Gateway.

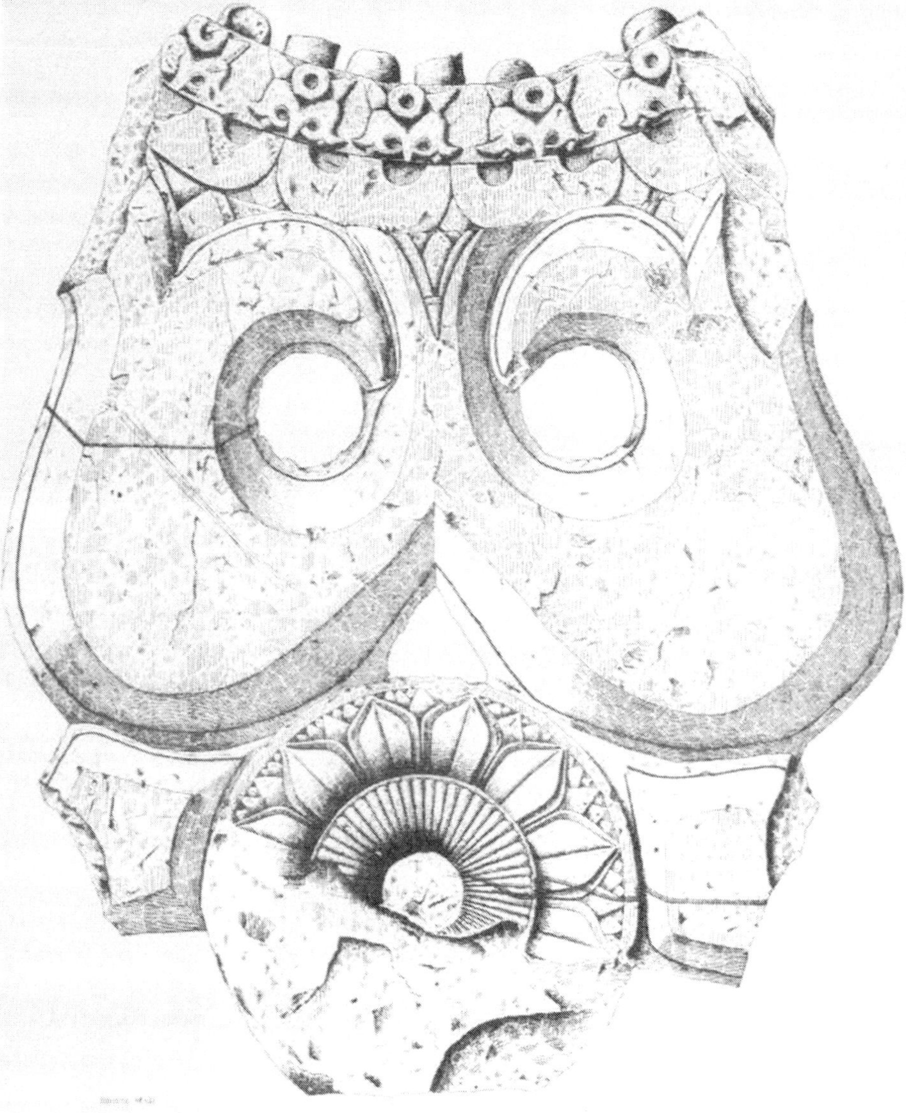

Front Elevation

Side Elevation.

Scale of Feet

Inches 12 9 6 3 1 Foot

DETAILS OF DECORATIVE ORNAMENTS

FRONT ELEVATION.

Fig. 1.

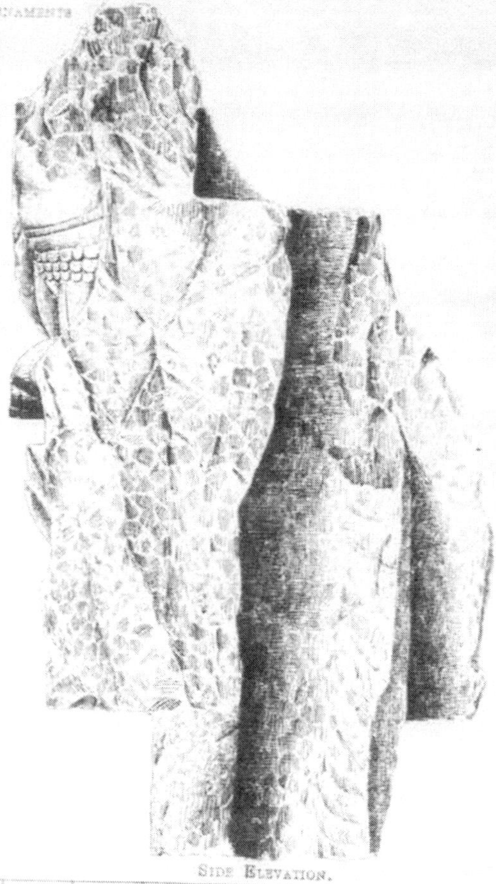

SIDE ELEVATION.

Fig. 2

FRONT ELEVATION

SECTION.

INCHES 12 9 6 3 SCALE OF FEET 1 FOOT

MATHURA SERIES.—KANKÂLÎ TÎLÂ.

Details of Decorative Ornaments.

CHAPTER XI.—DECORATIVE DETAILS.

PLATES XXXVIII(a), XXXIX, XL, XLI, AND XLII.

DECORATIVE DETAILS.

THE details illustrated in Plate **XXXVIII(a)** have been already dealt with in the descriptions of other plates. Small variations do not require detailed notice.

The fragments of sculpture illustrated in Plate **XXXIX** were evidently good work, but are too much damaged to be of value.

The object represented in Plate **XL** is the pinnacle of a *torana* gateway. The elements in the design are the wheel and *triratna*. The picture of a *torana* in Plate **XII** *ante*, shows how such pinnacles were used.

Plate **XLI** gives examples of different patterns of perforated windows. Specimens of elaborately-carved drains or spouts are given in Plate **XLII**.

The monstrous crocodile with a fish tail in figure 1 is executed with spirit. The fish shown in figure 2 swimming away from a pursuer is not so successfully executed.

A fish is, according to some lists, the emblem of Âranâtha, the eighteenth Jina.

CHAPTER XII.—PILLARS AND CAPITALS.

PLATES XLIII TO LI.

PILLARS AND CAPITALS.

THE nine plates Nos. XLIII to LI may most profitably be examined and considered together. Detailed description is not necessary, as the plates explain themselves. But the reader's attention may be invited to a few points.

The capitals are extremely complex structures, consisting of a large number of members. The most noticeable feature is the introduction of a group of winged lions between the upper and lower capitals in many instances.

The shafts of the pillars figured in Plates XLIII and XLIV bear mason's marks in early characters, "A-II" and "A-IV" respectively.

The lower capital in Plate XLV has the reeded form which is familiar in the Aśoka pillars.

Plates XLVI, XLVII, and XLVIII offer examples of shafts highly decorated with all the exuberance of detail so dear to Indian art.

Detached lion capitals are illustrated in Plates XLIX and L.

The under-surface, or soffit, of the capital represented in Plate L is prettily decorated with a simple leaf pattern.

Plate LI gives some further details of individual members of two capitals.

MATHURA SERIES.—KANKÂLÎ TÎLÂ.

DETAILS OF PILLAR.

SIDE ELEVATION

FRONT ELEVATION.

PLAN.

SCALE OF FEET

INCHES 12 9 6 3 0 1 2 FEET

DETAILS OF PILLAR.

SIDE ELEVATION.

FRONT ELEVATION.

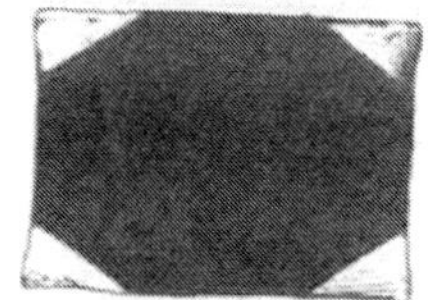

PLAN.

INCHES 12" 9 6 3 SCALE OF FEET 1 2 FEET

MATHURA SERIES.—KANKÂLÎ TÎLÂ. PLATE XLV

DETAILS OF PILLAR.

SIDE ELEVATION.

FRONT ELEVATION.

PLAN.

MATHURA SERIES.—KANKÂLÎ TÎLÂ.

DETAILS OF PILLARS.

Photo-zincographed at the Survey of India Offices, Calcutta, October [illegible]

DETAILS OF CORNER PILLAR AND SPIRAL COLUMN.

Photo-zincographed at the Survey of India Offices, Calcutta, October

MATHURA SERIES.—KANKÂLÎ TÎLÂ.

PLATE XLVIII.

DETAILS OF PILLARS AND SPIRAL COLUMN.

Capitals of Gateway Pillars

Fig. 1.

Side Elevation.

Front Elevation.

Fig. 2.

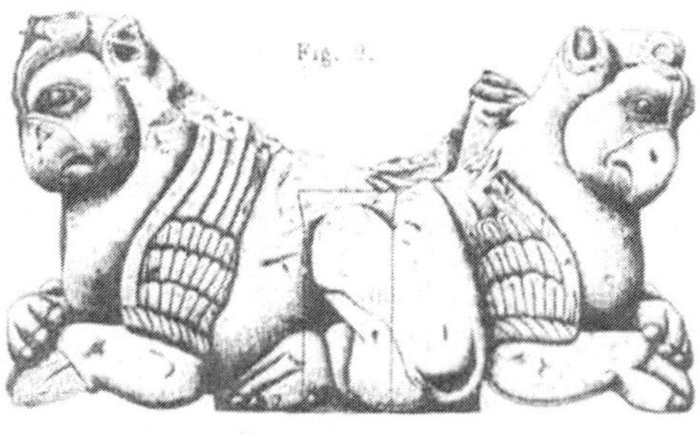

Front Elevation.

Side Elevation.

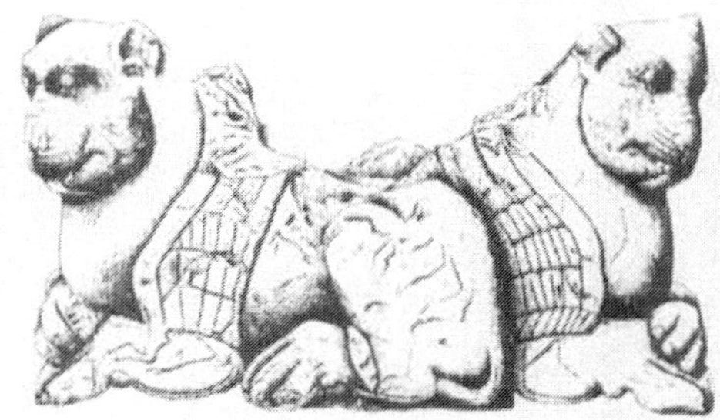

Back Elevation.

Scale of Feet

Inches 12 9 6 3 0 1 2 3 Feet

Photozincographed at the Survey of India Offices, Calcutta, October 18[illegible]

MATHURA SERIES.—KANKALI TILA.

CAPITAL OF GATEWAY PILLAR.

Fig. 1.

SIDE ELEVATION. FRONT ELEVATION.

Fig. 2.

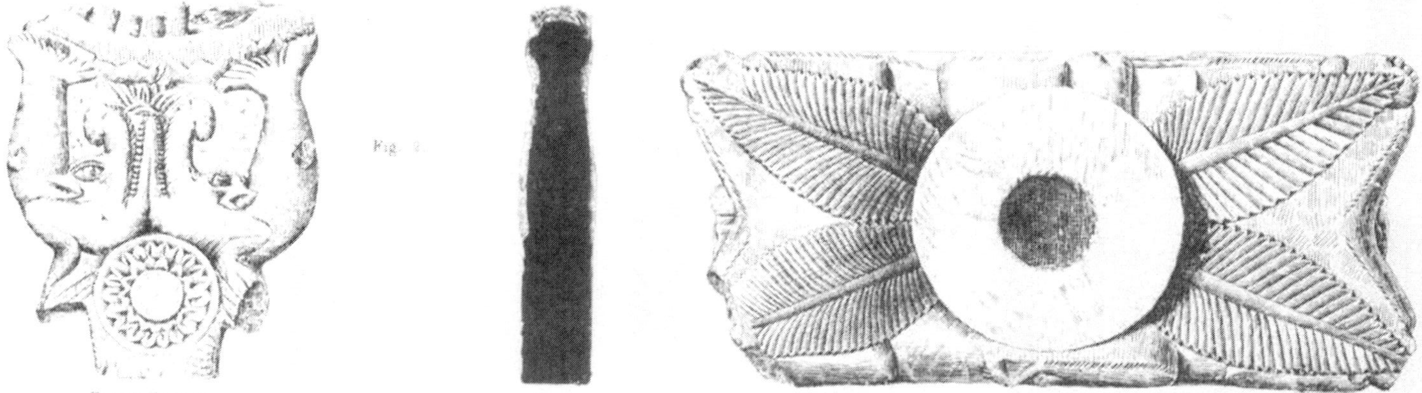

FRONT ELEVATION. SECTION. UNDER-SURFACE ELEVATION.

PINNACLE OF GATEWAY.

SCALE OF FEET

INCHES 12 9 6 3 0 1 2 3 FEET

MATHURA SERIES.—KANKÂLÎ TÎLÂ. PLATE LI.

DETAILS OF CAPITALS.

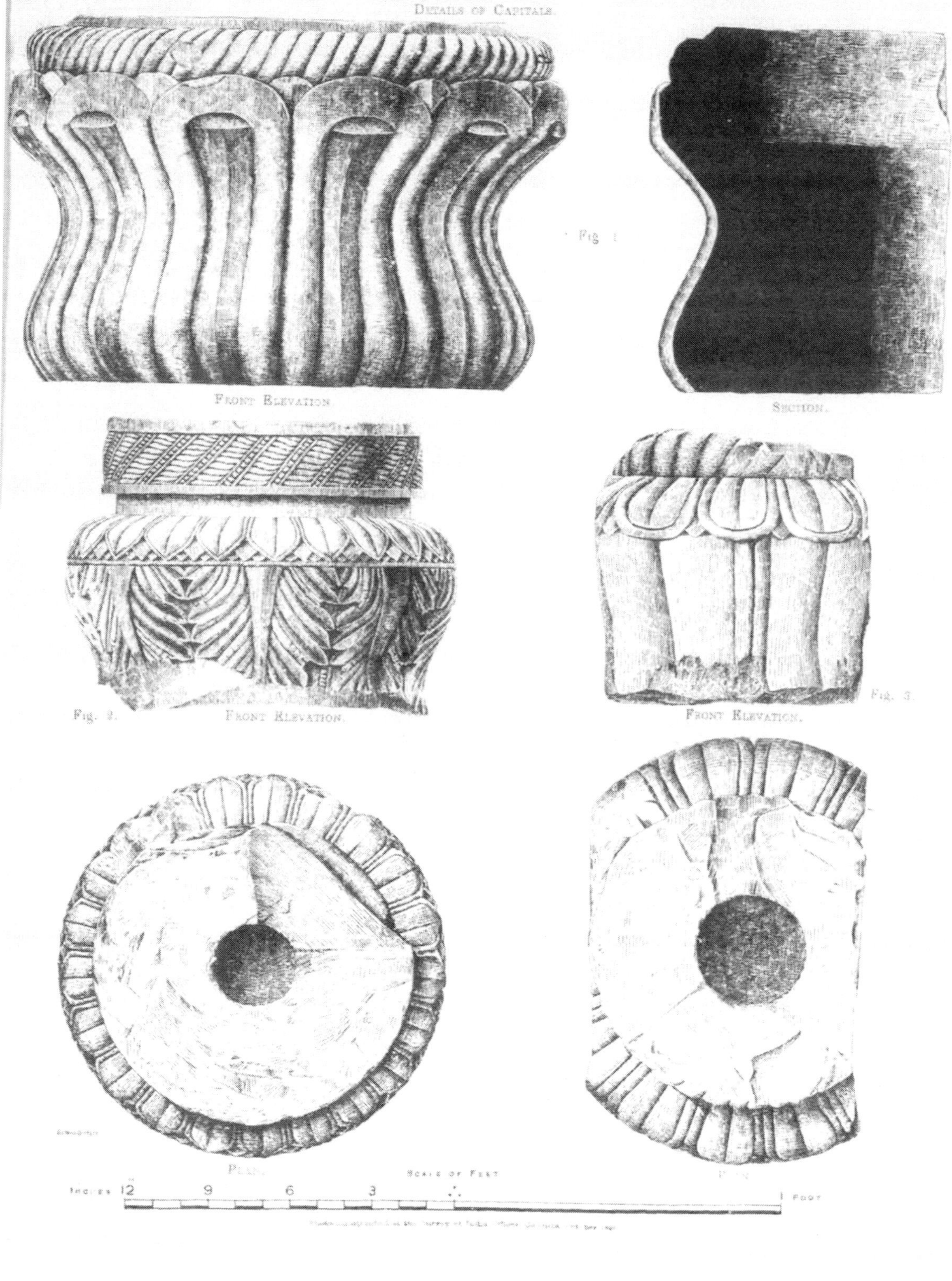

Fig. 1. FRONT ELEVATION. SECTION.

Fig. 2. FRONT ELEVATION. PLAN.

Fig. 3. FRONT ELEVATION. PLAN.

PLATE LIX.

MATHURA SERIES.—KANKÂLÎ TÎLÂ.

DETAILS OF CORNER RAILING PILLAR.

MATHURA SERIES.—KANKÂLÎ TÎLÂ.

PLATE LVIII.

DETAILS OF RAILING PILLARS.

MATHURA SERIES.—KANKÂLÎ TÎLÂ.

DETAILS OF RAILING PILLARS.

PLATE LVI.

MATHURA SERIES.—KANKÂLÎ TÎLÂ. PLATE LV.

DETAILS OF RAILING PILLAR.

MATHURA SERIES.—KANKÂLÎ TÎLÂ.

DETAILS OF RAILING PILLARS.

PLATE LIII.

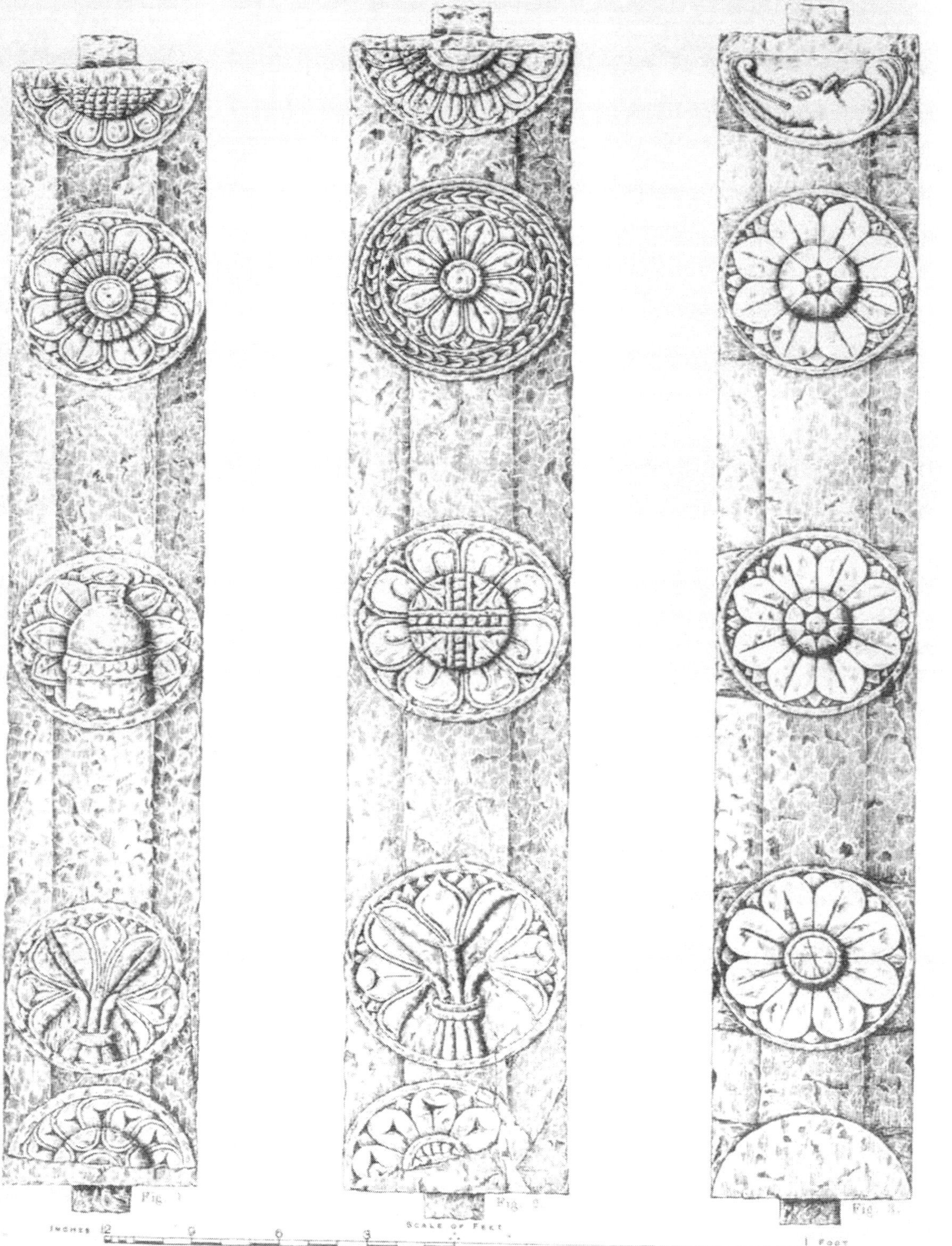

Details of Railing Pillars.

Fig. 1. Fig. 2. Fig. 3.

Scale of Feet

Inches 12 9 6 3 0 1 Foot

Photo-zincographed at the Survey of India Offices, Calcutta, October [illegible]

CHAPTER XIII.—RAILING PILLARS.

PLATES LII TO LIX.

RAILING PILLARS WITHOUT HUMAN FIGURES.

THIS series of plates gives ample, and indeed more than adequate, illustrations of the pillars of the railings round a *Stûpa* or *Stûpas*, such as are familiar to all students of Indian antiquities. Hitherto pillars of this class have been known only from Buddhist sites, and the term " Buddhist railing " has thus come into common use. The discovery of the Jain *Stûpa* in the Kankâlî mound makes this term unsuitable, and it is quite possible that some of the " Buddhist railings " discovered at other sites may turn out to be Jain. The decorations on the pillars in the present series are composed of the usual elements, and there is nothing distinctive about them to show whether the railing to which they belonged was Jain or Buddhist. But the buildings on the mound being principally Jain, the probability is that the railings were Jain also. The value of the excavations carried out by Dr. Führer and other gentlemen in the Kankâlî mound is much diminished by the failure to keep exact notes of the position and dimensions of the buildings exposed. If such notes had been recorded no doubt would have existed as to the building to which these railings belonged.

The side elevations in Plates LIV and LV show the lenticular holes into which the ends of the stone rails were fitted.

Some examples of stone railings have been fitted together and set up in the Lucknow Museum.

PLATES LX TO LXIV.

RAILING PILLARS WITH HUMAN FIGURES.

This series of pillars is more peculiar and interesting than the preceding series, and is, with the exception of Plate LXIV, undoubtedly Jain. The figures in Plates LX to LXIII are indecently naked and could not be Buddhist. With the exception of one male figure in an obscene attitude in Plate LXIII, all these naked figures are female and seem to be intended for dancing-girls. The costume, if such it may be called, consists solely of jewellery and an ornamental girdle round the hips.

The figures stood on the front elevation, the reverse elevation being decorated with ornaments of the usual rosette types.

The trees under which the women stand are in each case of a distinct kind. I cannot venture to identify the trees.

In Plate LX and LXI the women stand on crouching grotesque dwarfs, and wear enormous cylindrical ornaments in their ears.

In Plate LXII the woman carries a mace in her left hand, and stands on a ledge, beneath which are two conventional lions.

In Plate LXIII the woman stands on a plinth marked with a peculiar trefoil ornament. The male figure in Plate LXIV wears an elaborate headdress, and is decently clothed. He seems to be intended for a princely personage, or a Bodhisattva. The pillar illustrated in this plate may be either Jain or Buddhist.

MATHURA SERIES.—KANKÂLÎ TÎLÂ.

Details of Railing Pillar

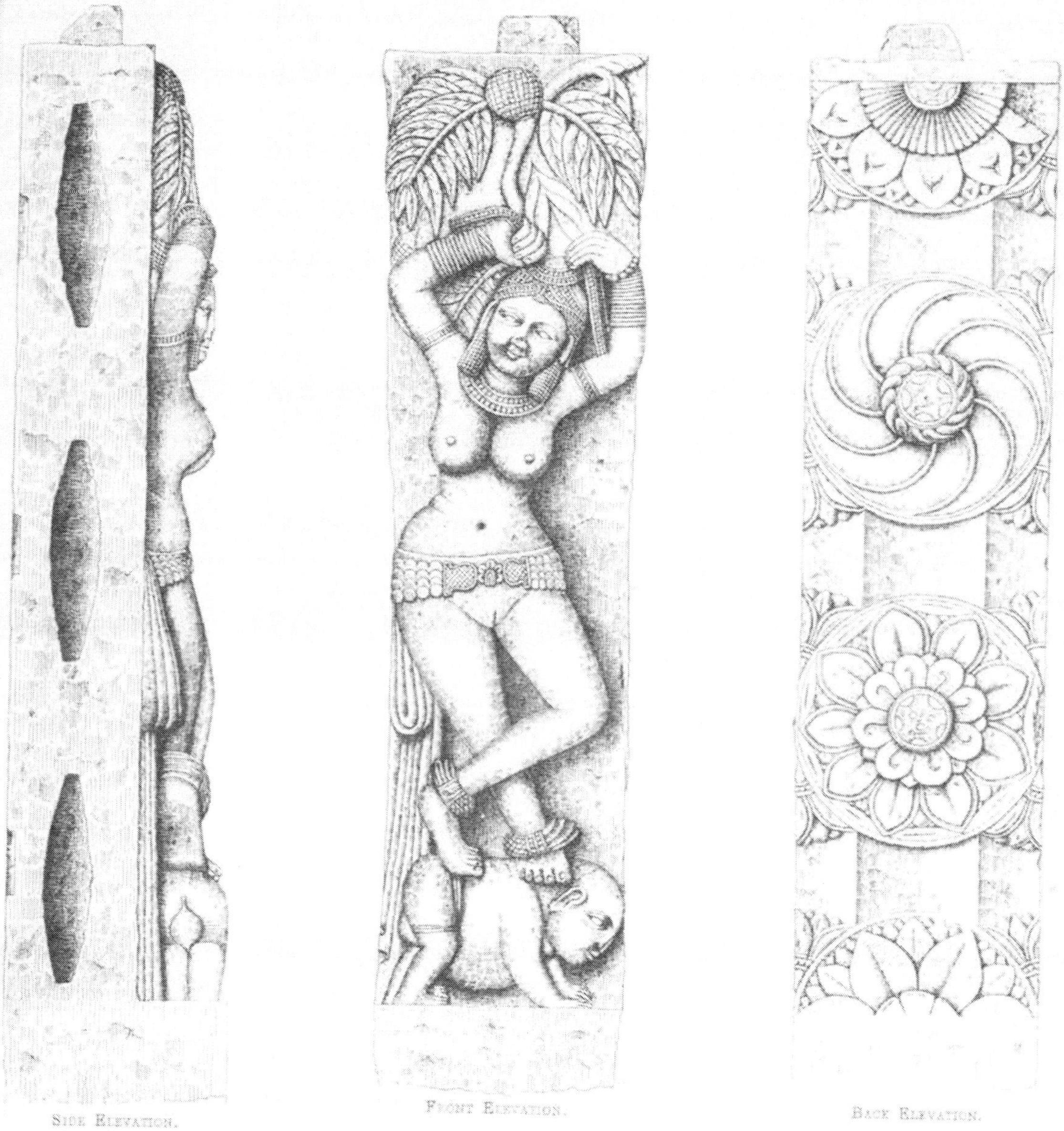

Side Elevation. Front Elevation. Back Elevation.

Scale of Feet

Inches 12 9 6 3 Foot

Photo-zincographed at the Survey of India Offices, Calcutta, October [illegible]

MATHURA SERIES.—KANKÂLÎ TÎLÂ.

DETAILS OF RAILING PILLAR.

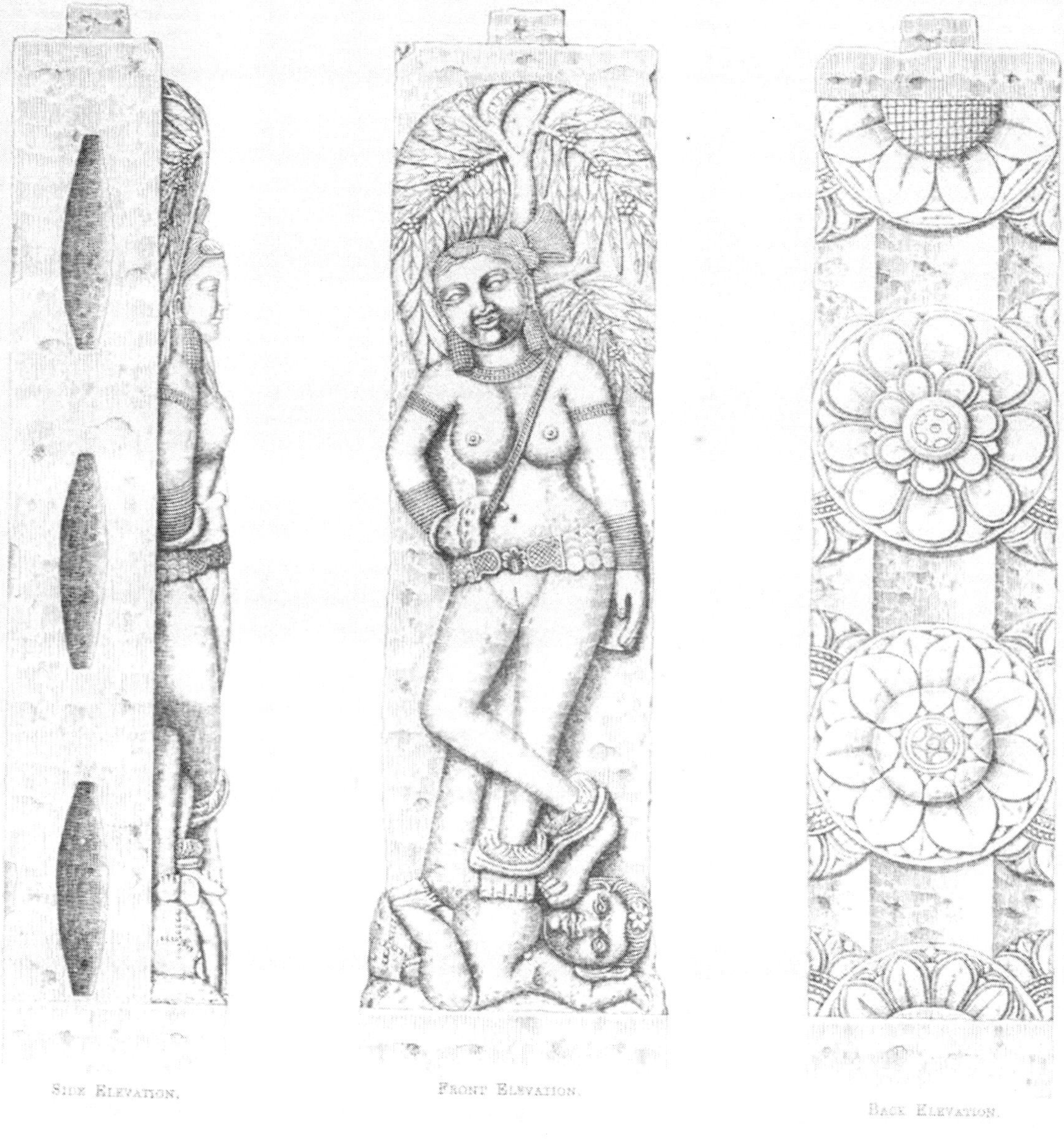

SIDE ELEVATION.

FRONT ELEVATION.

BACK ELEVATION.

SCALE OF FEET

INCHES 12 9 6 3 1 FOOT

Photo-zincographed at the Survey of India Offices, Calcutta, [illegible]

Details of Railing Pillar.

Side Elevation. Front Elevation. Back Elevation.

Photo-zincographed at the Survey of India Offices, Calcutta, October [illegible]

MATHURA SERIES.—KANKÂLÎ TÎLÂ.

DETAILS OF RAILING PILLAR.

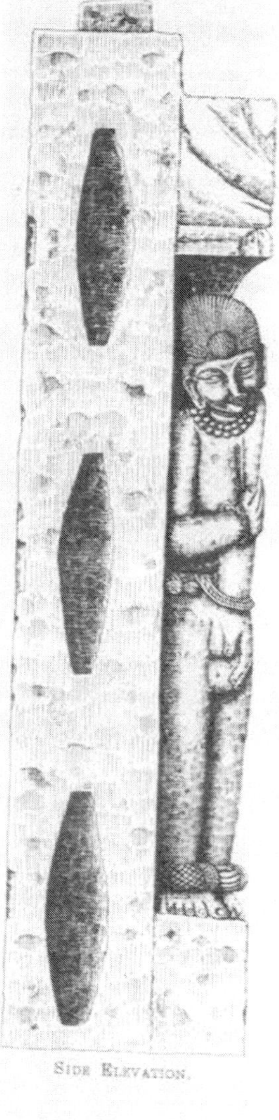

SIDE ELEVATION.

FRONT ELEVATION.

BACK ELEVATION.

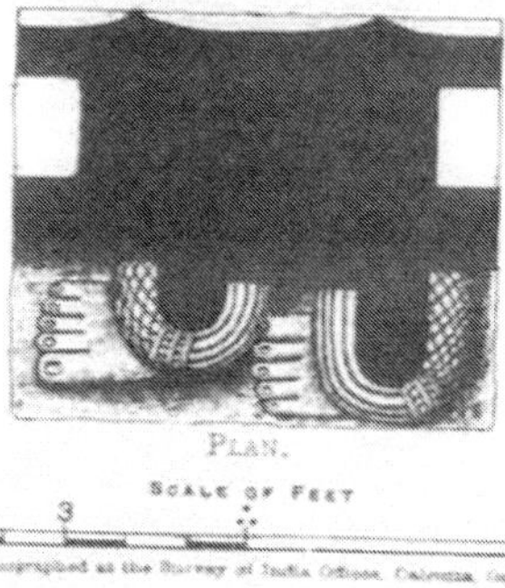

PLAN.

SCALE OF FEET

INCHES 12 9 6 3 0 1 FOOT

Photo-zincographed at the Survey of India Offices, Calcutta, October 18[illegible]

Details of Railing Pillar.

Front Elevation.

Side Elevation.

Back Elevation.

Scale of Feet

Inches 12 9 6 3 0 1 Foot

Photo-zincographed at the Survey of India Offices, Calcutta, October

MATHURA SERIES.—KANKĀLĪ TĪLĀ.

DETAILS OF RAIL-BARS.

Fig. 1.

FRONT ELEVATION. SECTION. BACK ELEVATION.

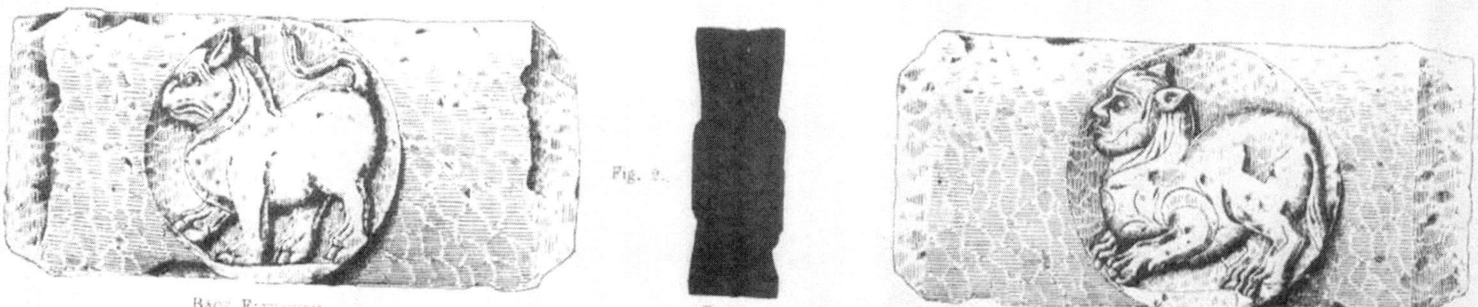

Fig. 2.

BACK ELEVATION. SECTION. FRONT ELEVATION.

SCALE OF FEET

INCHES 12 9 6 3 0 1 FOOT

MATHURA SERIES.—KANKÂLÎ TÎLÂ.

DETAILS OF RAIL-BARS.

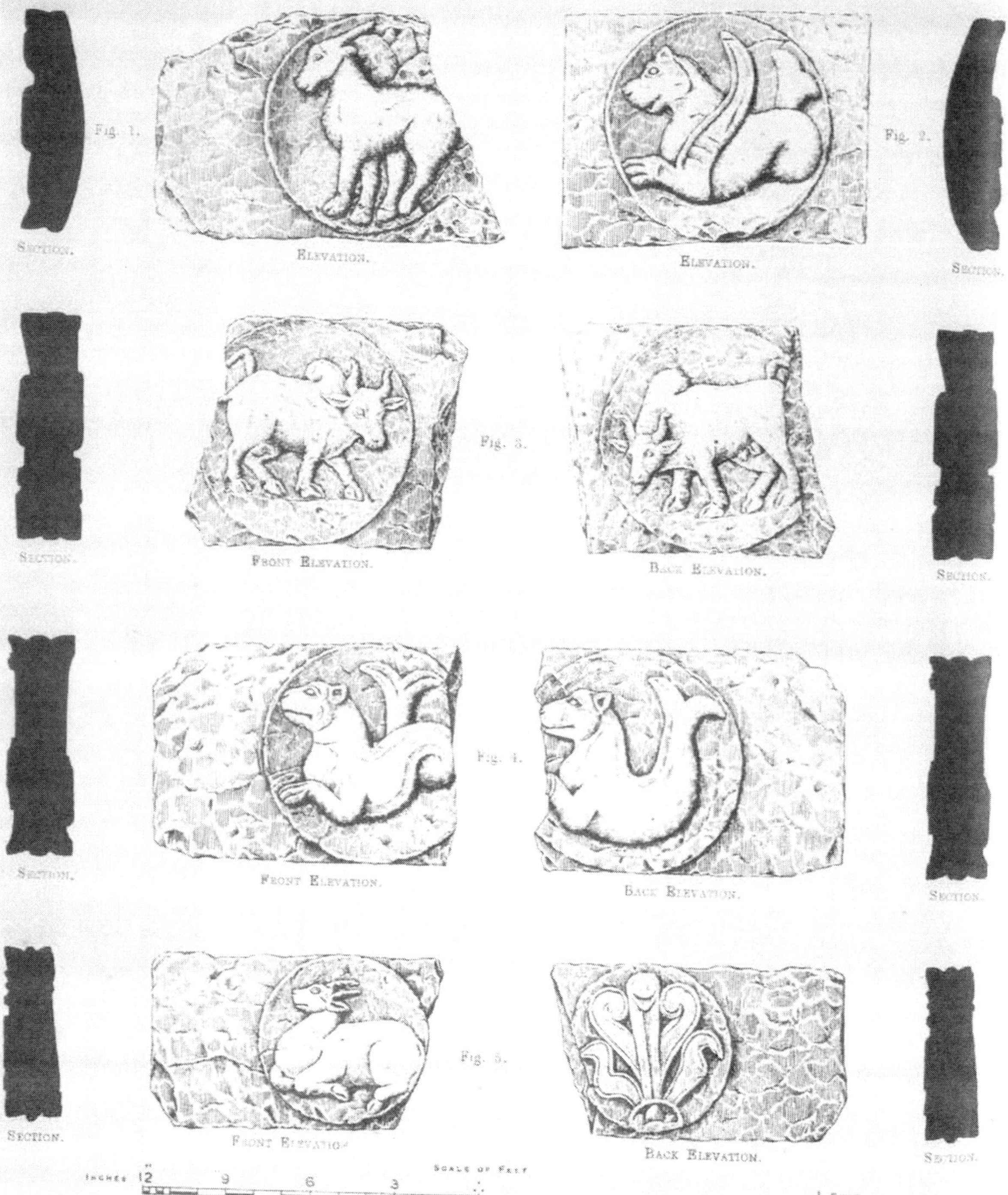

Photo-lithographed at the Survey of India Offices, Calcutta, October [illegible]

MATHURA SERIES.—KANKÂLÎ TÎLÂ.

DETAILS OF RAIL BARS.

Fig. 1.

Fig. 2.

Fig. 3.

Fig. 4.

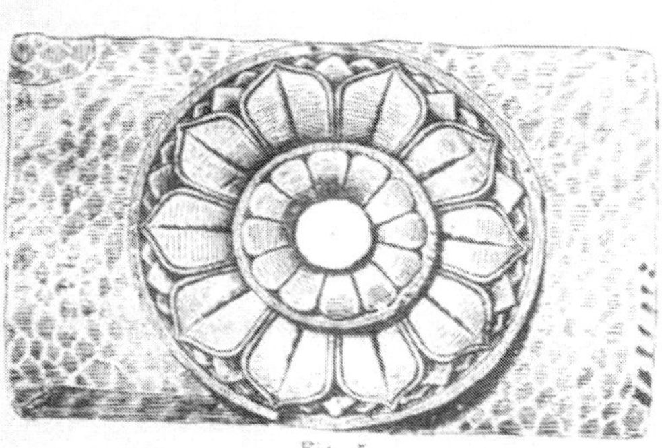

Fig. 5.

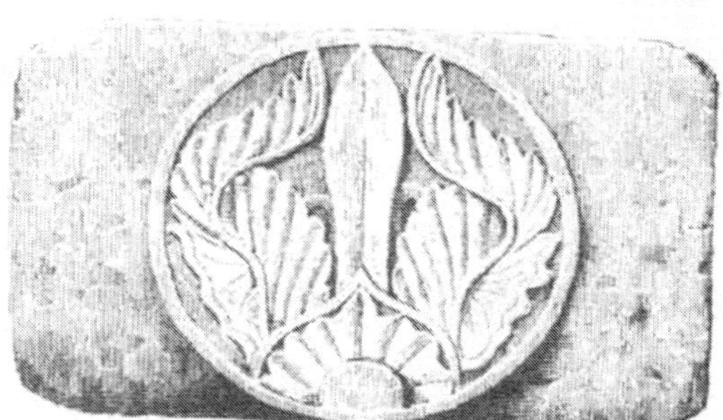

Fig. 6.

SCALE OF FEET

INCHES 12 9 6 3 0 1 FOOT

Photo-zincographed at the Survey of India Offices, Calcutta, October 18…

DETAILS OF RAIL-BARS.

Fig. 1.

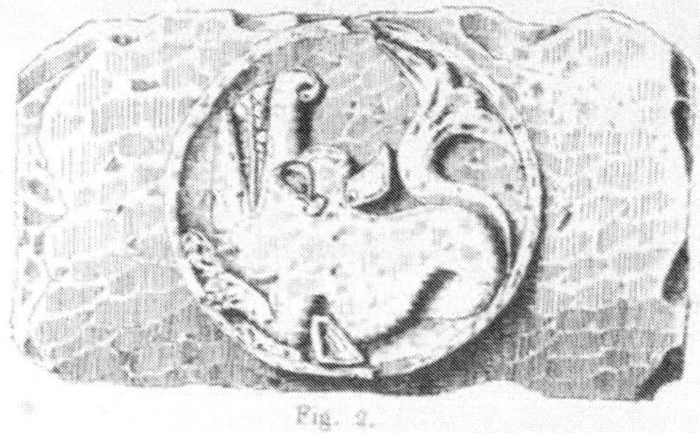

Fig. 2.

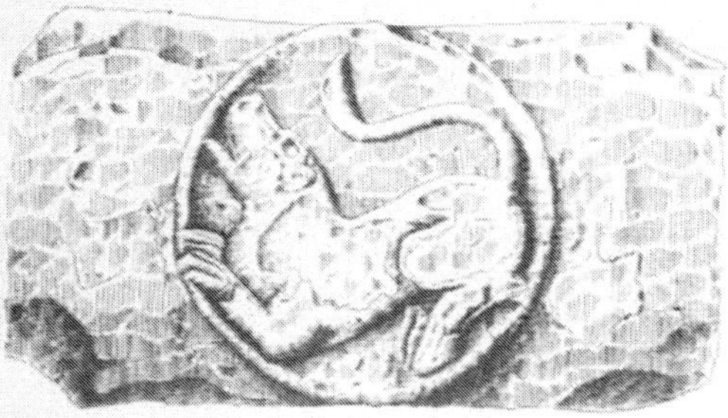

Fig. 3.

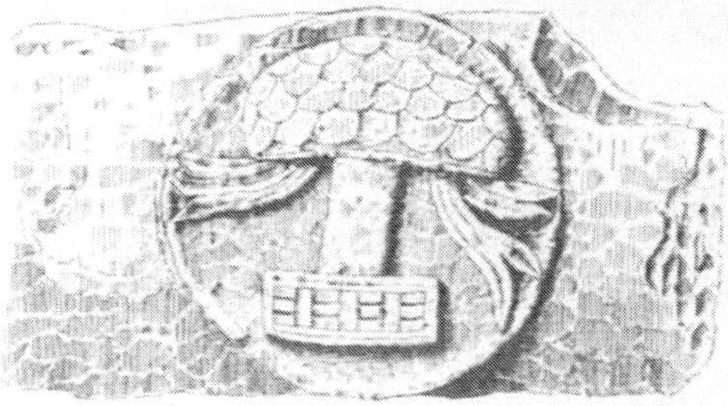

Fig. 4.

Fig. 5.

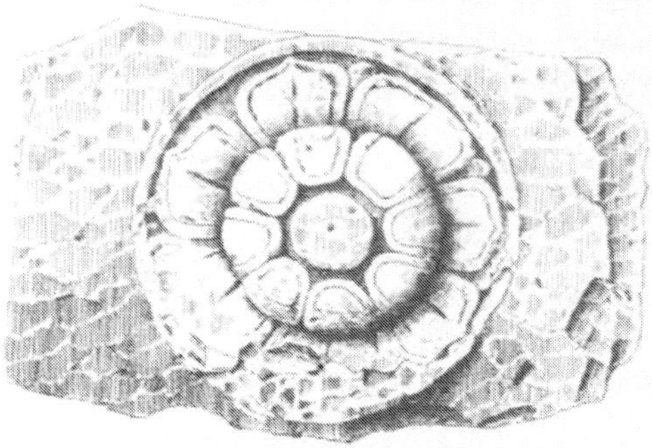

Fig. 6.

Fig. 7.

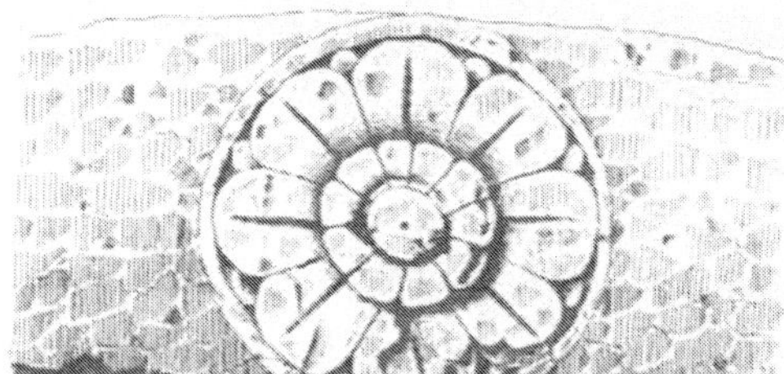

Fig. 8.

SCALE OF FEET

INCHES 12" 9 6 3 0 1 FOOT

MATHURA SERIES.—KANKÂLÎ TÎLÂ.

DETAILS OF RAIL-BARS. PLATE LXXII.

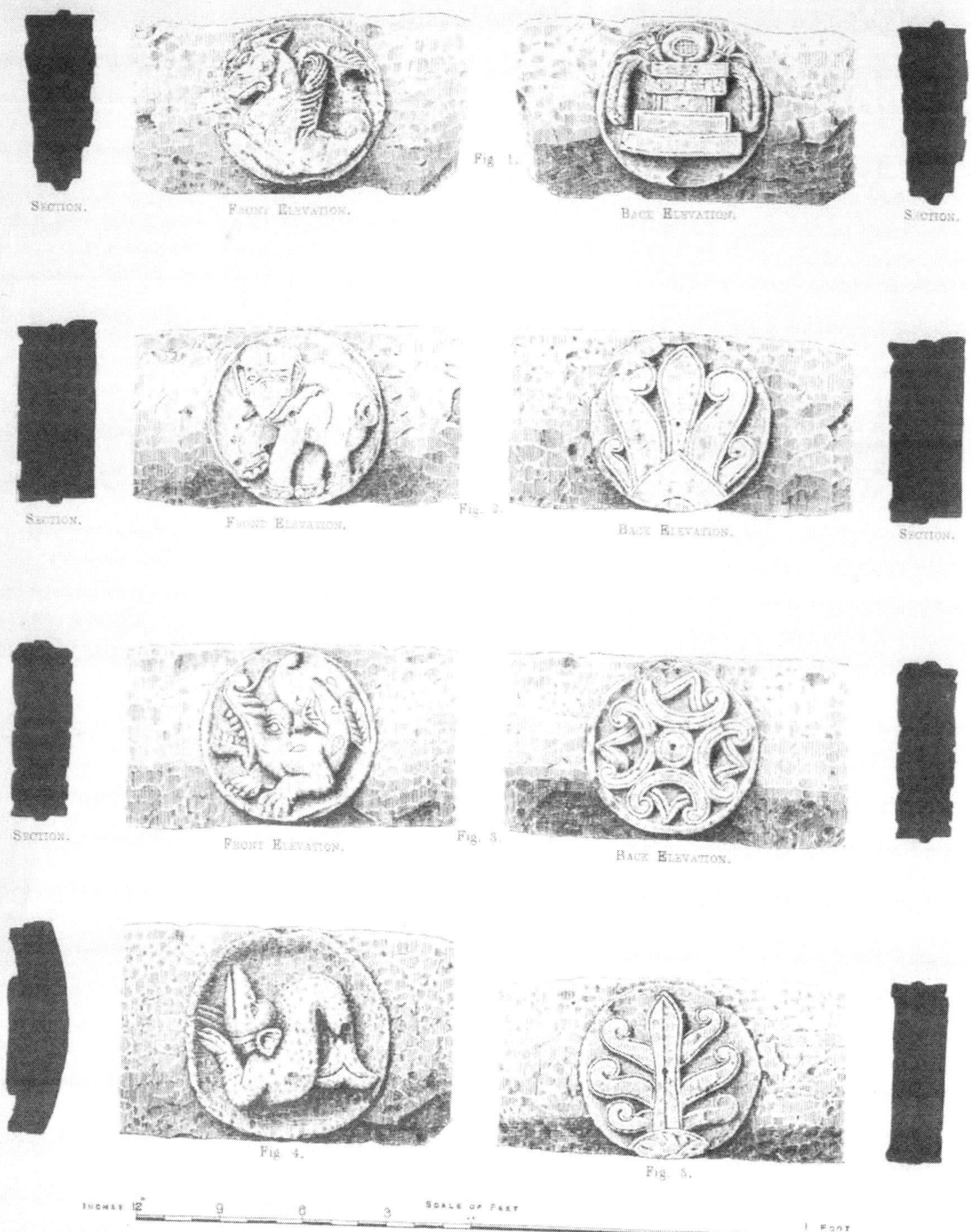

Photo-zincographed at the Survey of India Offices, Calcutta, October [illegible]

MATHURA SERIES.—KANKÂLÎ TÎLÂ.

PLATE LXXI.

DETAILS OF RAIL-BARS.

MATHURA SERIES.—KANKĀLĪ TĪLĀ.

Details of Rail-Bars.

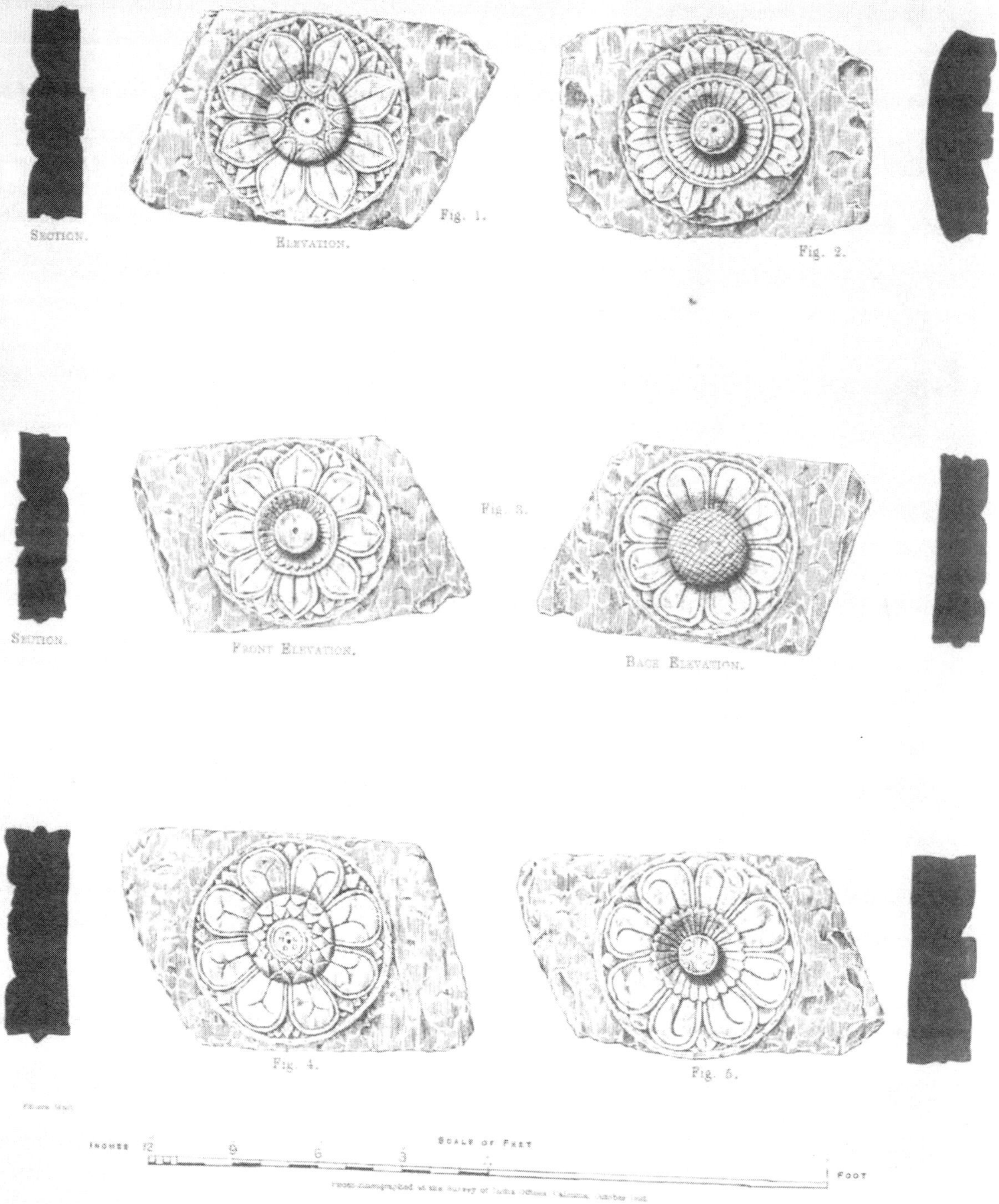

MATHURA SERIES.—KANKÂLÎ TÎLÂ.

DETAILS OF RAIL-BARS.

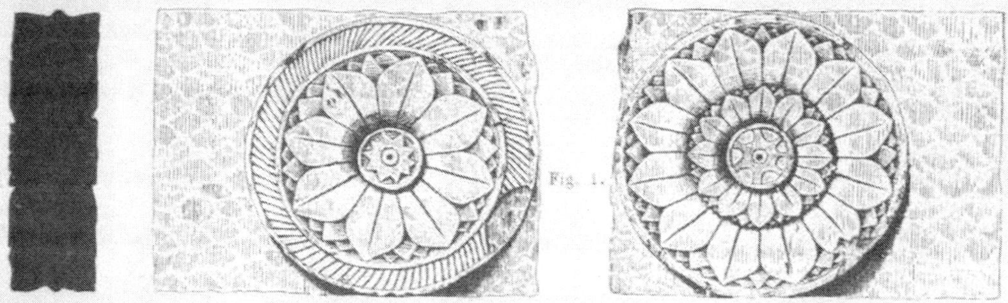

SECTION. FRONT ELEVATION. Fig. 1. BACK ELEVATION.

Fig. 2.

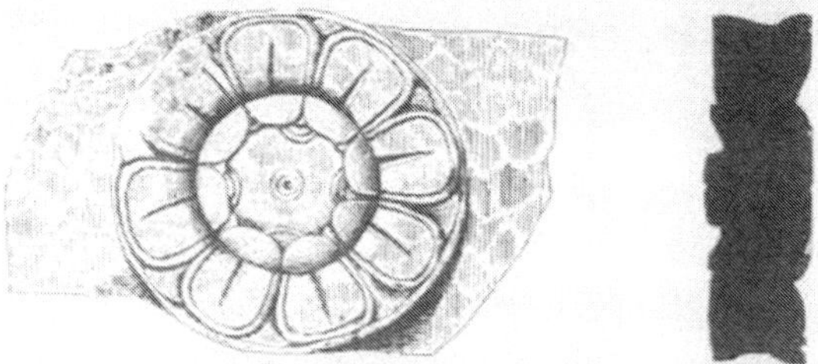

Fig. 3.

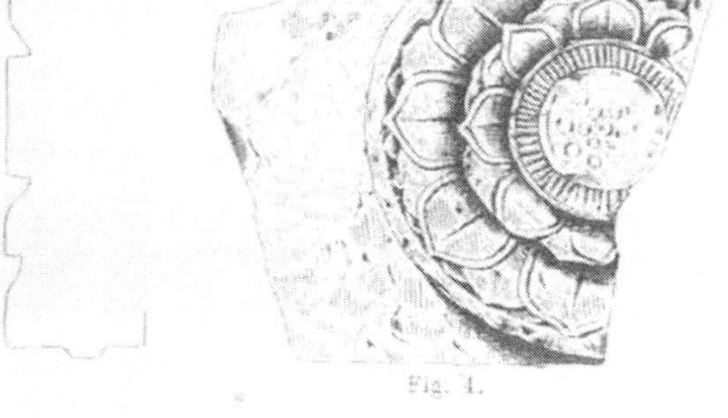

Fig. 4.

Fig. 5.

SCALE OF FEET

INCHES 12 9 6 3 0 1 FOOT

Photo-zincographed at the Survey of India Offices, Calcutta, October

MATHURA SERIES.—KANKÀLÎ TÎLÂ.

PLATE LXVIII.

DETAILS OF RAIL-BARS.

Fig. 1.

Fig. 2.

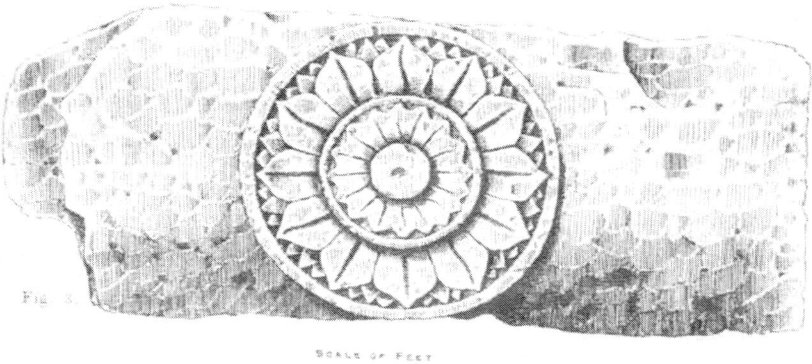

Fig. 3.

SCALE OF FEET

INCHES 12 9 6 3 1 FOOT

Photo-lithographed at the Survey of India Offices, Calcutta, October [illegible]

MATHURA SERIES.—KANKÂLÎ TÎLÂ.

Details of Rail-Bars.

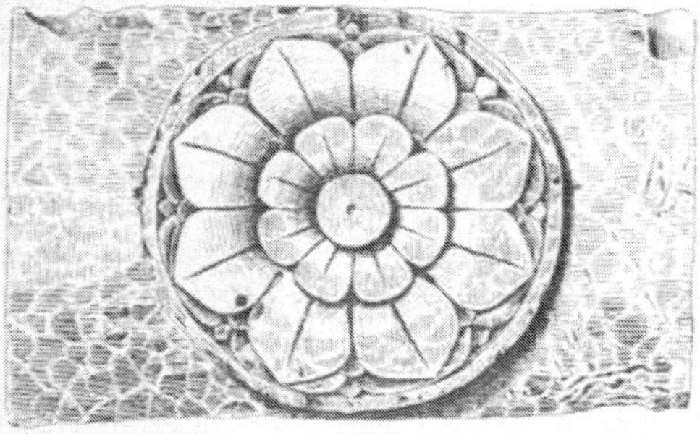

Back Elevation.

Fig. 1.

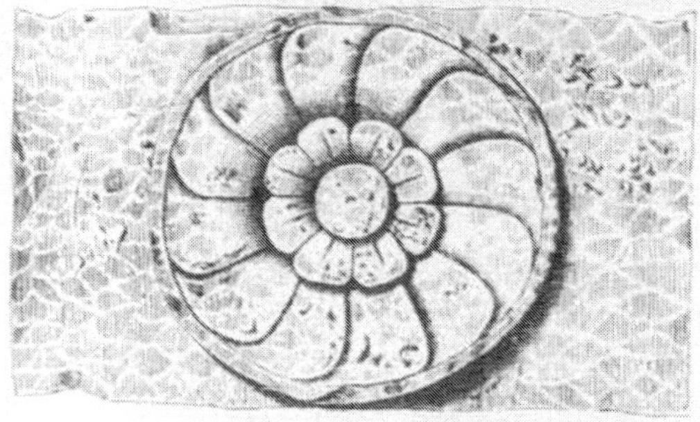

Front Elevation.

Back Elevation.

Fig. 2.

Front Elevation.

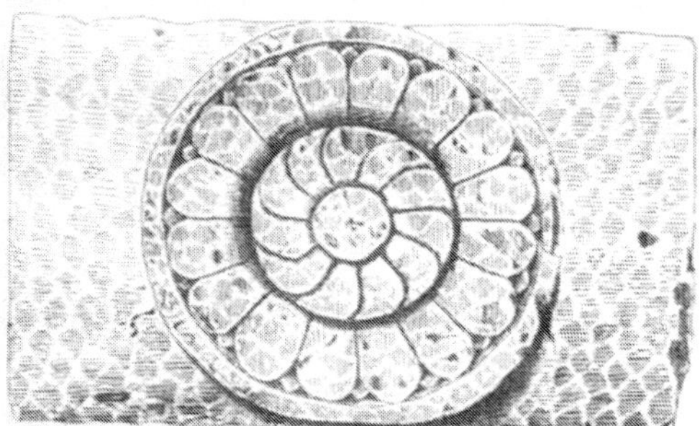

Front Elevation

Fig. 3

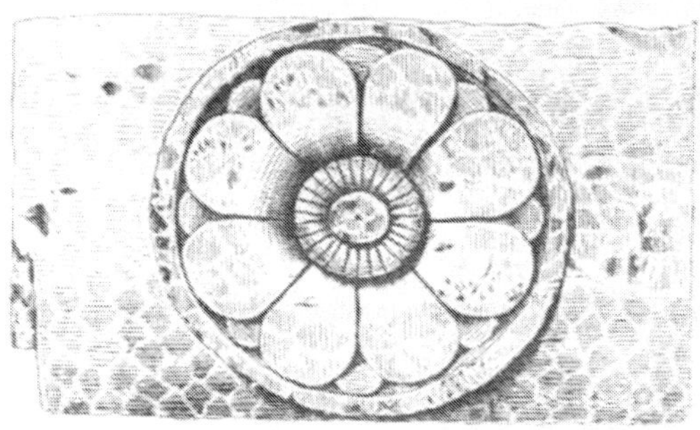

Back Elevation.

Inches 12 9 6 3 — Scale of Feet — 1 Foot

Photo-zincographed at the Survey of India Offices, Calcutta, October 1885.

MATHURA SERIES.—KANKÂLÎ TÎLÂ.

DETAILS OF RAIL-BARS.

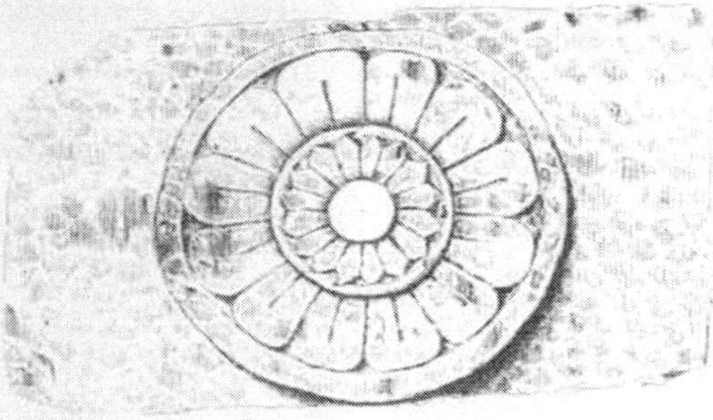

FRONT ELEVATION.

Fig 1.

BACK ELEVATION.

Fig. 2.

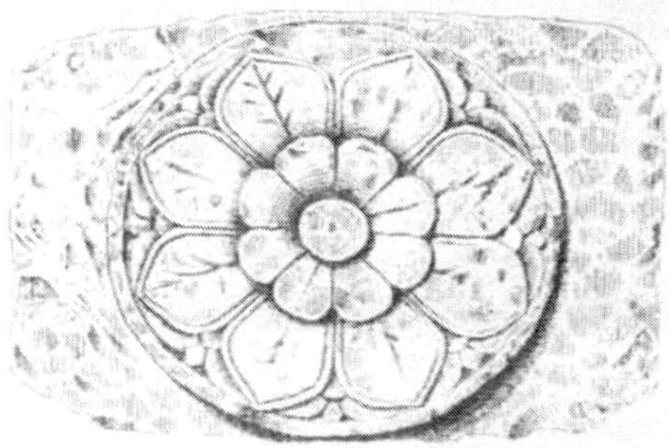

Fig. 3.

FRONT ELEVATION.

Fig. 4.

BACK ELEVATION.

SCALE OF FEET

INCHES 12 9 6 3 0 1 FOOT

Photo-zincographed at the Survey of India Offices, Calcutta, October [illegible]

Details of Rail-Bars.

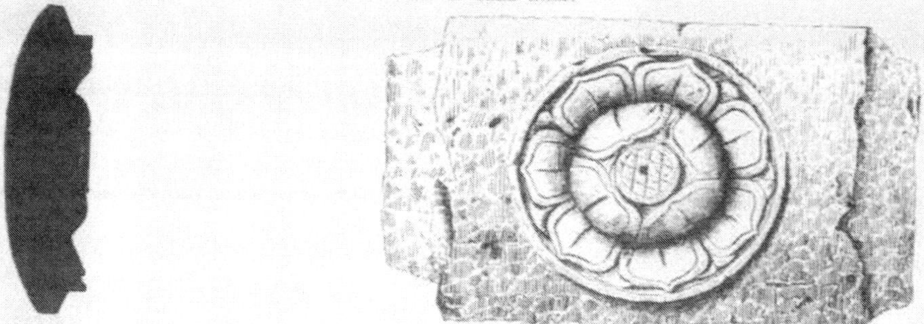

Section. Front Elevation.

Fig. 1.

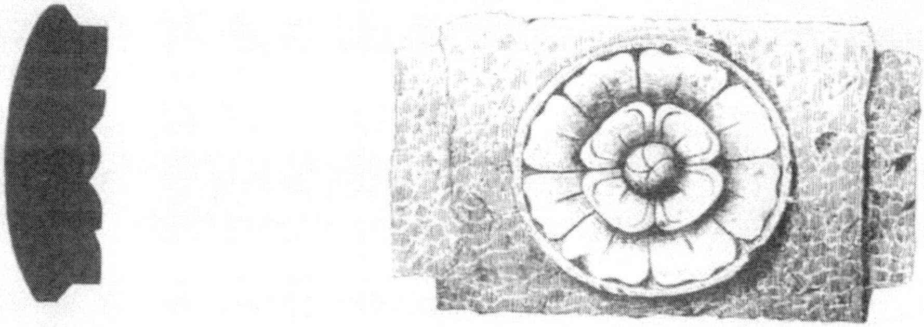

Fig. 2.

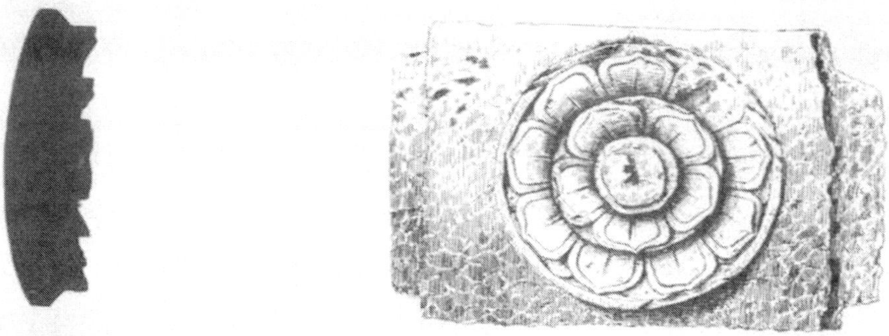

Fig. 3.

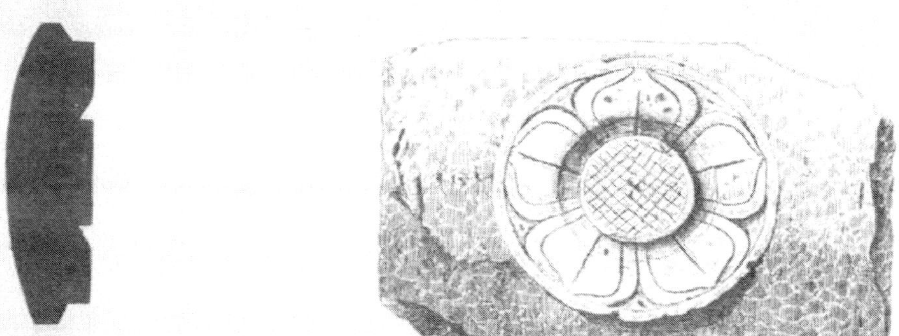

Fig. 4.

Inches 12 9 6 3 Scale of Feet 1 Foot

Photo-zincographed at the Survey of India Offices, Calcutta, October [illegible]

CHAPTER XIV.—ORNAMENTAL BOSSES ON RAILINGS.

PLATES LXV TO LXXVI.

ORNAMENTAL BOSSES ON RAIL BARS.

This series might have been abridged with advantage.

The ornaments figured in Plates LXV to LXX are not remarkable, except for their variety.

Cleverly-designed winged lions and other monsters are shown in Plate LXXI, figures 2 and 8; Plate LXXII, figures 3 and 4; Plate LXXIII, figures 1, 2, and 3; Plate LXXIV, figures 1 and 4; and Plate LXXVI.

The elegance of the leaf patterns in figure 3 of Plate LXXI and figure 6 of Plate LXXIV deserves notice.

The shell in figure 7 of Plate LXXI is an unusual ornament. It is the emblem of Neminâtha, the twenty-second Jina, or Tîrthaṁkara.

The edifice shown in figure 1 of Plate LXXII (back elevation) seems to be a peculiar kind of *Stûpa* or pedestal built in horizontal tiers. The heavy sausage-shaped garlands are similar to those worn by the seated Jina in Plate VII.

A sacred tree inside a railing adorned with streamers is depicted in figure 4 of Plate LXXIII.

Elephants in different positions are shown in figure 2 of Plate LXXII and figure 2 of Plate LXXIV.

A goose is delineated in figure 3 of Plate LXXIV, and antelopes and bulls are shown in Plate LXXV.

The elephant is the emblem of Ajitanâtha, the second Jina; the goose is the emblem of Sumatinâtha, the fifth Jina; and the antelope is the emblem of the sixteenth Jina, Śântinâtha.

CHAPTER XV.—COPING-STONES AND PEDIMENTS.

PLATES LXXVII TO LXXXIV.

DETAILS OF COPING-STONES OF RAILINGS, AND A PEDIMENT.

In many instances the motive of the lower member of the decoration is a wavy band or garland, similar to that borne by men or boys in many Buddhist sculptures and in the central band of the *Toraṇa* in Plate XIX. The upper member frequently consists of a combination of a row of bells with a beaded ornament.

Examples of deeply undercut foliage are seen in figure 3 of Plate LXXVII and figure 1 of Plate LXXVIII. In the last-named example the combination of a grotesque animal's head with the foliage is very clever.

Bounding antelopes are shown in figure 3, Plate LXXVIII and figure 3, Plate LXXXII.

In Plate LXXIX, figure 2, a tiger is pursuing a pig. Plate LXXX, figure 3, gives a good representation of a rhinoceros; and a buffalo is shown in figure 1, Plate LXXXI.[1]

Seated Jinas form part of the decoration in figure 1, Plate LXXXII. The female seated in a dormer window, in Plate LXXXIII, figure 1, resembles that in Plate XXXII.

The objects depicted in figure 2, Plate LXXXIII and figure 1, Plate LXXXIV, are not coping-stones, but fragments of the pediment of a steeple.

Plate LXXXII has been already published as Plate 87 of the "Journal of Indian Art and Industry" for October 1893, Volume V, No. 44.

[1] The rhinoceros is the emblem of Śrī Ananatha, the eleventh Jina: the buffalo is the emblem of Vasupadya, the twelfth Jina.

Details of Coping Stones.

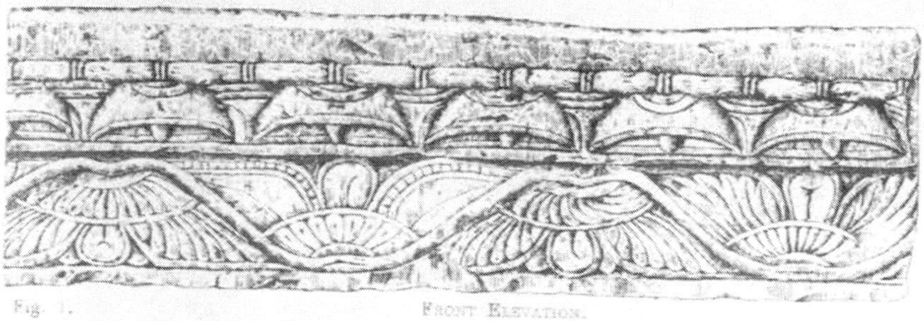

Fig. 1. Front Elevation.

Section.

Fig. 2. Front Elevation.

Section.

Fig. 3. Front Elevation.

Section.

Scale of Feet

Inches 12 9 6 3 0 1 Foot

Photo-lithographed at the Survey of India Offices, Calcutta, October

Details of Coping Stones.

Fig. 1.
Front Elevation.

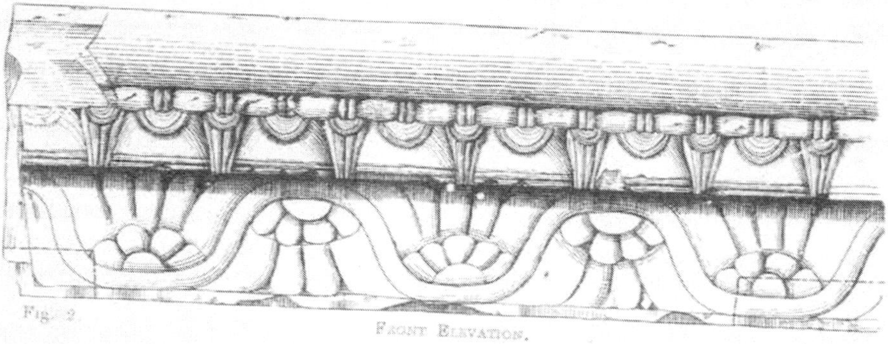

Fig. 2
Front Elevation.

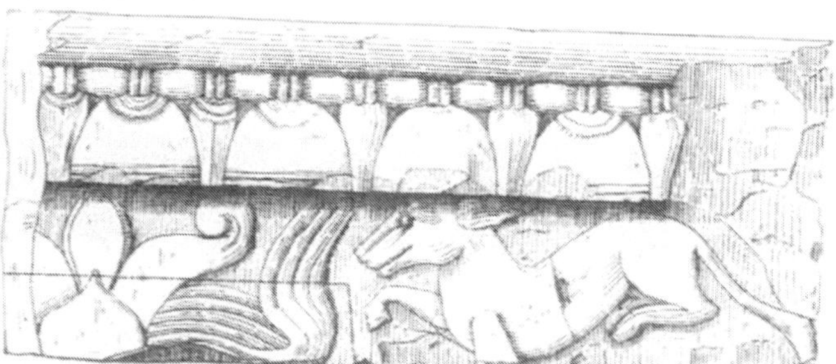

Fig. 3.
Front Elevation.

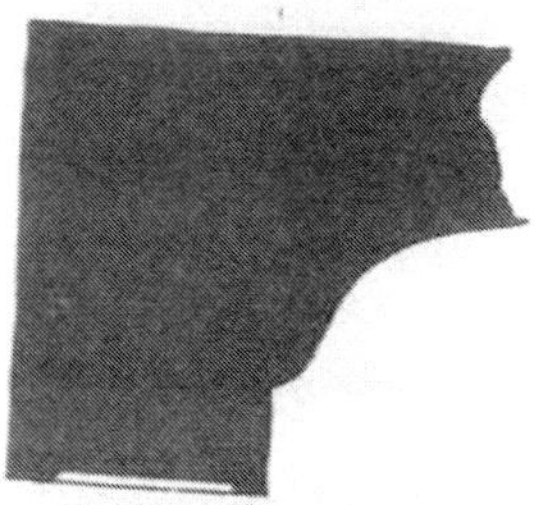

Section.

Section.

Section.

Photo-zincographed at the Survey of India Offices, Calcutta, October [illegible]

MATHURA SERIES.—KANKÂLÎ TÎLÂ

DETAILS OF COPING STONES.

Fig. 1. FRONT ELEVATION.

SECTION.

Fig. 2. FRONT ELEVATION.

BACK ELEVATION.

SCALE OF FEET

INCHES 12 9 6 3 0 1 FOOT

Photo-zincographed at the Survey of India Offices, Calcutta, [illegible]

PLATE LXXX.

MATHURA SERIES.—KANKÂLÎ TÎLÂ

Details of Coping Stones.

Section. Fig. 1. Front Elevation.

Section. Fig. 2. Front Elevation.

Section. Fig. 3. Front Elevation.

Scale of Feet

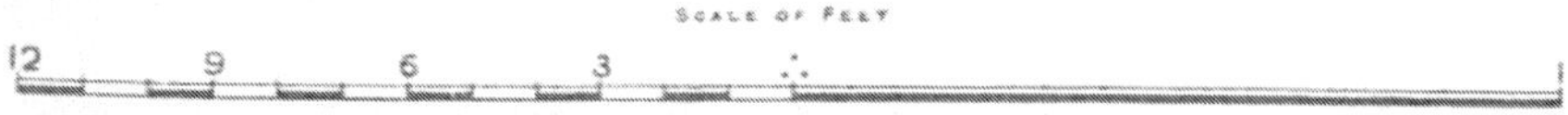

MATHURA SERIES.—KANKĀLĪ TĪLĀ

DETAILS OF COPING STONES.

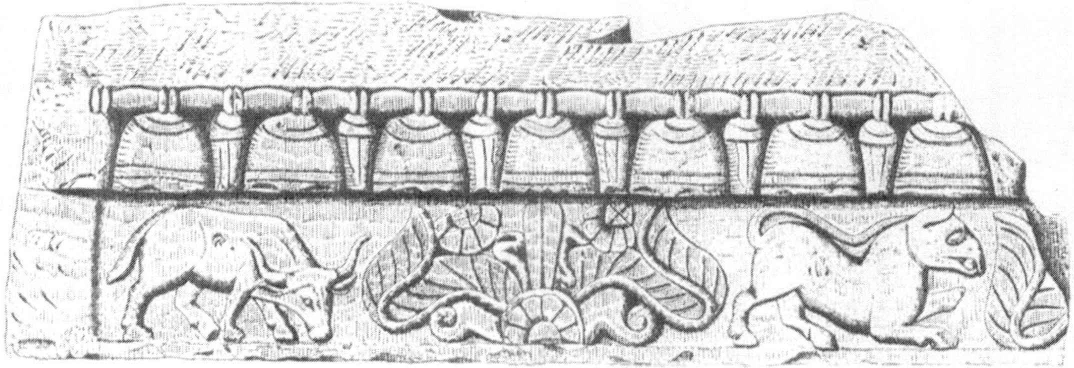

Fig. 1. FRONT ELEVATION. SECTION.

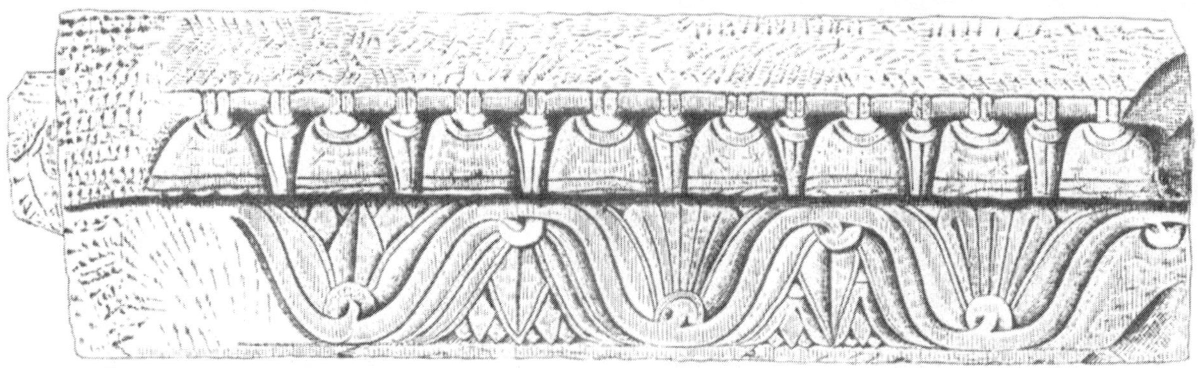

Fig. 2. FRONT ELEVATION. SECTION.

SCALE OF FEET

INCHES 12" 9 6 3 0 1 FOOT

Photo-zincographed at the Survey of India Offices, Calcutta, October 1900.

MATHURA SERIES.—KANKÂLÎ TÎLÂ

Details of Coping Stones.

Back Elevation. Side Elevation.

Fig. 1.

Front Elevation. Side Elevation.

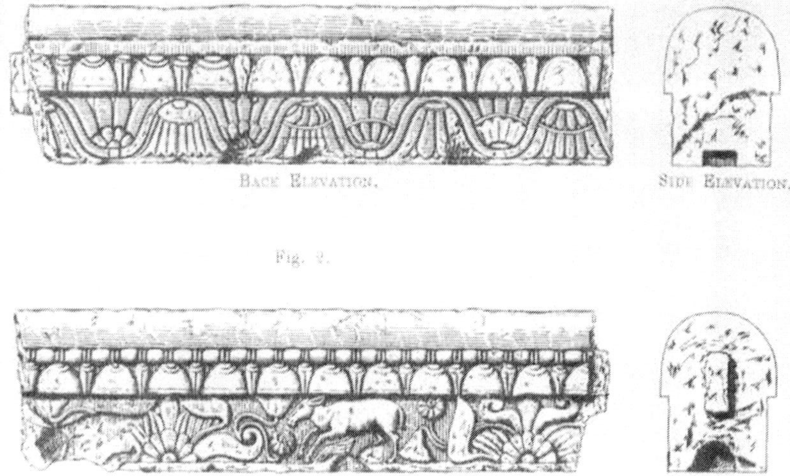

Back Elevation. Side Elevation.

Fig. 2.

Front Elevation. Side Elevation.

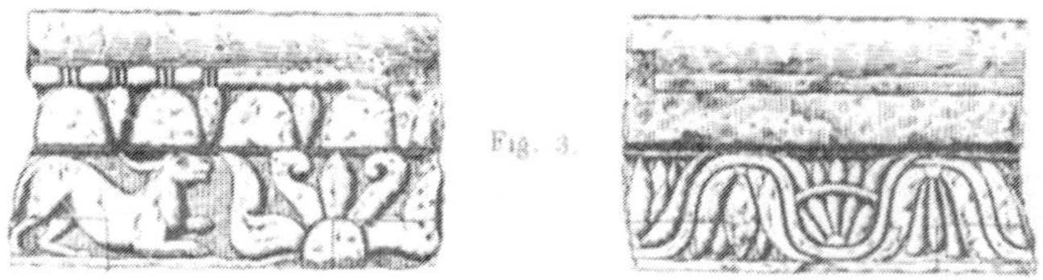

Back Elevation. Fig. 3. Front Elevation.

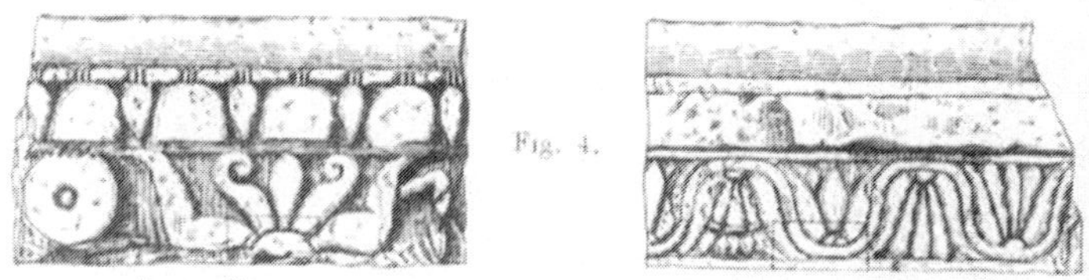

Front Elevation. Fig. 4. Back Elevation.

Photo-lithographed at the Survey of India Offices, Calcutta, October 1901.

FRONT ELEVATION.
SECTION.
Fig. 1.
BACK ELEVATION.
SECTION.
Fig. 2.
FRONT ELEVATION.
SECTION.
SCALE OF FEET
INCHES 12 9 6 3 1 FOOT

PLATE LXXXIV.

MATHURA SERIES.—KANKĀLĪ TĪLĀ.

DETAILS OF COPING STONES.

SECTION. Fig. 1. FRONT ELEVATION.

SECTION. Fig. 2. FRONT ELEVATION.

SCALE OF FEET

INCHES 12 9 6 3 0 1 FOOT

Photo-lithographed at the Survey of India Offices, Calcutta, [illegible]

MATHURA SERIES.—KANKÂLÎ TÎLÂ.

SCULPTURED PANEL REPRESENTING VARDHAMÂNA SEATED UNDER THE BODHI TREE.

INCHES 6 3 SCALE OF FEET 1 FOOT

Photo-zincographed at the Survey of India Offices, Calcutta, October

CHAPTER XVI.—A SEATED SAINT.

PLATE LXXXV.

A SEATED SAINT.

THE panel represented in this plate is said to have been found to the south of the shrine of Kankâlî. It is in an imperfect state of preservation, and the inscription, which probably was recorded on the base, has been wholly lost.

Dr. Führer labels the plate as a "sculptured panel representing Vardhamâna seated under the Bodhi tree." But for this description no justification exists. No Bodhi tree is represented. The panel simply has a leaf and stem border on the right and left sides. I am unable to find any indication that the personage represented is intended for Vardhamâna, or Mahâvîra, the twenty-fourth and last of the Jain Tîrthaṁkaras. The sign of Vardhamâna was a lion, and of such sign there is no trace.

Plates XCI and XCIV, *post*, give examples of undoubted images of Vardhamâna, with his lion cognizance in each case. Those images are, as usual, nude. The figure of the saint in the tablet under discussion is decently clothed, as are all his attendants. In reality it is impossible to identify the subject of the plate, or even to assert confidently that it is Jain. Dr. Führer himself declares that the remains in the Kankâlî mound included those of a Buddhist *vihâra* and of a Vaishnava temple in addition to the more prominent Jain edifices. So far as I can perceive, the sculpture in Plate LXXXV does not possess any distinctive Jain character. Mr. Mukherji suggests that the principal personage may be intended for Krishna. All that can be said at present with certainty is that the composition represents a seated saint receiving the homage of his adherents. The saint has a large halo and a headdress which suggests a snake's hood. He is seated on a pedestal composed of four slabs of stone, which may be compared with the pedestal or *Stûpa* of five tiers shown in Plate LXXII, 1. The disciple on each side is clothed like his master, and wears a similar headdress.

In the group of five disciples below the pedestal, only one, the largest figure, wears the same headdress. The three other male figures to the right seem to have their hair tied up in a topknot. The figure on the left is that of a woman.

CHAPTER XVII.—SUNDRY SCULPTURES.

PLATE LXXXVI.

FRAGMENTS OF SCULPTURE.

THE headdress of figure 1 is noticeable.

The spirited delineation of a buffalo in figure 2 is probably from a coping-stone of a railing. Compare Plate LXXXI.

The meaning of the mutilated group in figure 3 is not apparent. The large male holds a staff in his left hand, which may be the handle of an umbrella held over a lost seated figure. Two diminutive figures, one certainly female, and the other perhaps male, appear over the woman's left shoulder. The group seems to refer to some legend, which might be Jain, Buddhist or Brahmanical.

MATHURA SERIES.—KANKÂLÎ TÎLÂ.

FRAGMENTS OF SCULPTURED PANELS.

SIDE ELEVATION.

Fig. 1.

FRONT ELEVATION.

Fig. 2.

Fig. 3.

SCALE OF FEET

INCHES 12 9 6 3 0 1 FOOT

Photo-lithographed at the Survey of India Offices, Calcutta, [illegible]

MATHURA SERIES.—KANKĀLĪ TĪLĀ.

LIFE-SIZE STATUE OF VARDHAMĀNA TEACHING.

PLATE LXXXVII.

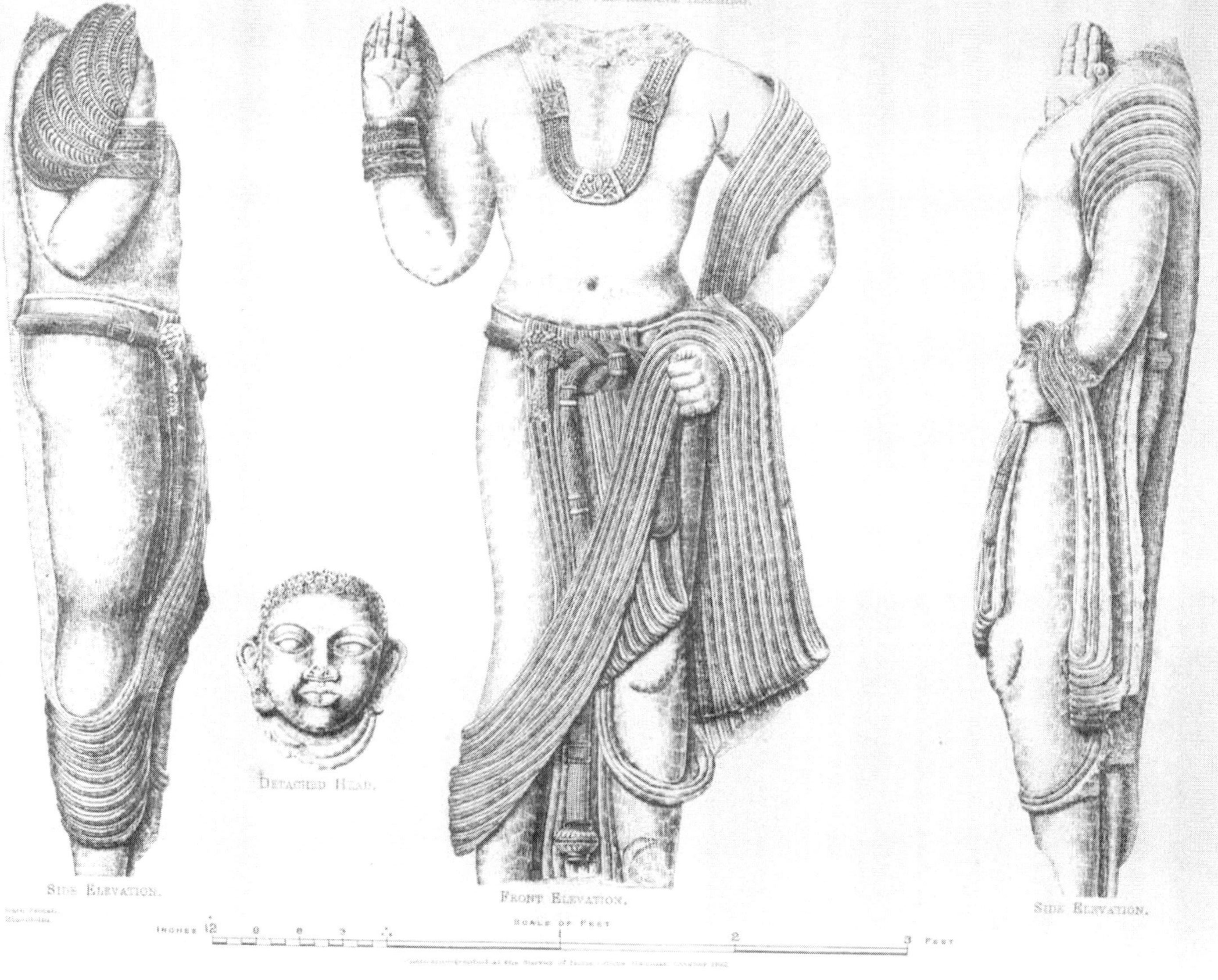

SIDE ELEVATION.

FRONT ELEVATION.

SIDE ELEVATION.

DETACHED HEAD.

SCALE OF FEET

INCHES 12 9 6 3 0 1 2 3 FEET

PLATE LXXXVII.

LIFE-SIZE HEADLESS STATUE.

This handsome statue is labelled in the Lucknow Museum as one of Buddha, and the plate is entitled by Dr. Führer "Life-size statue of Vardhamâna teaching." So far as I can perceive, there is no warrant for either description. There is nothing specially Jain or Buddhist in the design or execution of the work. Mr. Mukherji suggests that the image may be intended for that of a deity of the Brahmanical pantheon, raising his hand in the act of blessing. The ornaments worn are rich, and the drapery is cleverly executed.

The statue does not come from the Kankâlî mound, but is said to have been found among the ruins of Ganeśvara about three miles north-west of Mathurâ.

PLATE LXXXVIII.

STATUE OF A BOY WITH AUREOLE OF FLAMES.

The face, hands, and feet of this curious work have unfortunately been lost. The proportions of the figure are, as Mr. Mukherji observes, those of a boy, who is clothed in a waistcloth, with a sheet *(châdar)* thrown over his left arm. The headdress is peculiar, and the upper part of the figure from the elbows upwards is surrounded by an aureole of flames.

I cannot guess the identity of the personage represented. Dr. Führer's description of the statue as being one of the Jain saint Vardhamâna appears to be wholly without justification.

MATHURA SERIES.—KANKÂLÎ TÎLÂ.

STATUE OF VARDHAMÂNA SURMOUNTED BY THE LAMBENT FLAME OF SANCTITY.

FRONT ELEVATION.

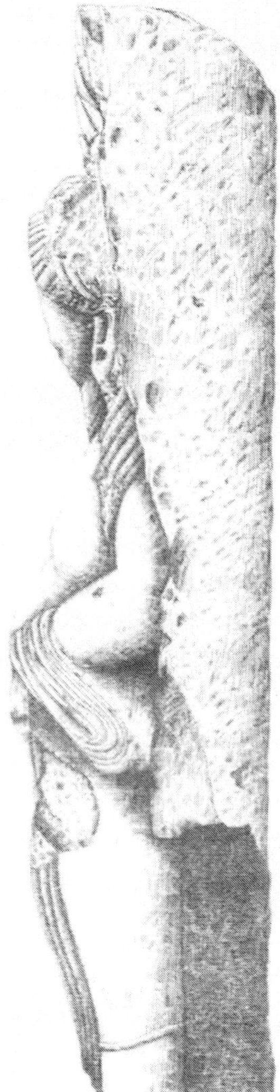

SIDE ELEVATION.

SCALE OF FEET

INCHES 12 9 6 3 0 1 FOOT

MATHURA SERIES.—KANKÂLÎ TÎLÂ.

STATUE OF ROYAL PERSONAGE.

SIDE ELEVATION.

FRONT ELEVATION.

SCALE OF FEET

INCHES 12 9 6 3 0 1 FOOT

[illegible] at the Survey of India Offices, Calcutta, October [illegible]

PLATE LXXXIX.

STATUE OF A ROYAL PERSONAGE (?)

The style of clothing and rich ornaments of this mutilated statue indicate that a person of high rank is represented. The right hand remains and rests on the thigh just above the knee. Long arms are a traditional attribute of the ideal king, and the length of the arm in this work justifies Dr. Führer's label of it as the statue of a royal personage.

No sectarian marks are visible, and the image may have formed part of the decoration of a Brahmanical temple. It is said to have been found in the Kankâlî mound.

CHAPTER XVIII.—QUADRUPLE JAIN IMAGES.

PLATE XC.

THREE QUADRUPLE IMAGES OF JAIN TÎRTHAṀKARAS.

THE sculptures illustrated in this plate are of more interest and importance than those treated of in the last few pages.

Figure 1.

This small work represents a quadruple image of an unnamed Jain saint, perfectly nude. It was found in the western part of the Kankâli mound, near the second, or Digambara, temple.

Dr. Bühler's transcription and translation of the inscription are as follows :—

A. 1. . . . . *Saṁ XV gṛi III di I asyâ purvv[â]ya*
B. 1. . . *hikâto kulâto aryya Jayabhûti*
C. 1. *sya śiśininaṁ aryya Saṅgamike śiśina—*
D. 1. *aryya Vasulaye [nirvartta]naṁ*
A 2. . . . *lasya dhi[tu]* . . . *i* . . *dhu veṇi—*
B. 2. *śreshṭi[sya] dharmapatniye Bhaṭṭi[se]nasya*
C. 2. . . . *[mâtu] Kumaramitayo danaṁ bhagavato [pra]—*
D. 2. *mâ sabbato bhadrikâ.*

" [*Success !*] In the year XV, in the third month of summer, on the first day, on that *(date specified as)* above, a fourfold image of the Divine one, the gift of Kumaramitâ *(Kumâramitrâ)*, daughter of . . . la, daughter-in-law of . . . , first wife of alderman *(śreshṭhin)* Veṇi, mother of Bhaṭṭisena, *(was dedicated at)* the request of the venerable Vasulâ, the female pupil of the venerable Saṅgamikâ, the female pupil of the venerable Jayabhûti out of the [*Me*]hika *Kula*."[1]

The lines shown in the plate are B.1, 2.

Bühler's translation of *Bhagavato* by the phrase "the Divine one" is not quite accurate. Jain saints were not regarded as gods, and the rendering "worshipful," or an equivalent, would be preferable.

The translation of *śreshṭhin* by "alderman" is also not convincing. I think it probable that the word meant "banker," the modern Seṭh.

The expression *pratimâ sabbato bhadrikâ*, "beautiful on all sides," is a technical term for a quadruple image.

The date and characters show that the image was dedicated in the reign of Kanishka. The year may be provisionally interpreted as approximately equivalent to A. D. 75.[2]

Figure 2.

This work closely resembles that depicted in figure 1, though the hair is differently treated.

The Jina shown in the plate is Pârśvanâth, the remains of his canopy of snake-hoods being discernible.

---

[1] "Epigraphia Indica," Vol. I, p. 382, No. II.

[2] I desire that stress may be laid on the words "provisionally" and "approximately." I am satisfied that the Kushân dates are not expressed in the Śaka era, and I agree with M. Boyer that the Saka era probably coincides with the accession of the Satrap Nahapâna in Western India, and that it originated in the West, not in the North, of India. See, *ante*, page 5, note 1. The assumption that the Kushân are began *about* A. D. 60 or 65 seems to fit the facts.

MATHURA SERIES.—KANKÂLÎ TÎLÂ

QUADRUPLE IMAGES OF TÎRTHAMKARAS.

Fig. 1.

Fig. 3.

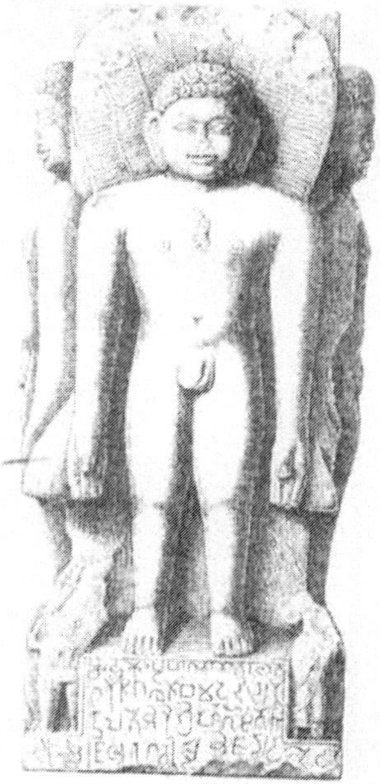

Fig. 2.

SCALE

INCHES 12 9 6 3 0 1 FOOT

Photo-zincographed at the Survey of India Offices, Calcutta, October 18[illegible].

The inscription, as read and translated by Bühler, is as follows :—

A. 1. *Siddha Ko[ṭṭi]yato gaṇato Uchena—*
2. *garito śakhato Bamhâdâsiato*
3. *kulato śirigrihato saṁbhokato*
4. *aryya Jeshṭahastisya śishyo a[ryya Mi]hi[lo]*

B. 1. *ttasya śishy[o] aryya Kshera*
2. *[ko] vâchako tasya nirvata—*
3. *na Vara[ṇa] hasti [sya]*

C. 1. *cha Deviya cha dhita jaya.—*
2. *devasya vadhu Moshiniye*
3. *vadhu Kuṭhasya Kamuthasya*

D. 1. *dhamrapa[ti]ha Sthirâê*
2. *dana savadobhadrika*
3. *sarvrasatvana hitasukhaye.*

"Success! The pupil of Ayyajeshṭahasti (*Jyeshṭhahastin*) out of the Koṭṭiya *gaṇa*, the Uchenagari (*Uchchânagarî*) Śakhâ, (*and*) the Bamhâdâsia (*Brahmadâsika*) *kula*, (*was*) Aryyamihila (*Ârya-Mihira*); his pupil (*was*) the preacher (*vâchako*) Arya-Ksheraka (*Ârya-Kshairaka?*); at his request a fourfold (*image was dedicated as*) the gift of Sthirâ, daughter both of Varaṇahasti (° *hastin*) and of Devî, daughter-in-law of Moshinî (*and*) first wife of Kuṭha Kasutha for the welfare and happiness of all creatures."[1]

The A face is shown in the plate.

The record is a capital example of the ill-spelled and ungrammatical composition which is common in this class of inscriptions. It is also a good example of a spiritual pedigree, and gives valuable details as to the constitution of the Jain church.

The inscription is not dated, but seems to be of approximately the same date as that shown in figure 1.

Mr. Mukherji notes that in the Lucknow Museum a wrong label is attached to the original.

Figure 3.

The work here figured is larger, and about a thousand years later in date than the sculptures just described. The style of Jain images is so conventional that the difference in age is not apparent from mere inspection. The fourfold image is that of Vardhamâna, whose lion cognizance is shown below his seat.

One side of the pedestal, not shown in the plate, is inscribed. The transcription and translation, according to Bühler, are as follows :—

L1. *Śrî Jinadevaḥ Sûristadanu Srî Bhâva devanâmâbhût âchârya Vijayasiṅga—*
2. *tachchhishyastena cha proktaiḥ sutrârakair Navagrâma Sthanâdisthai svasaktitaḥ*
3. *Vardhamânaśchaturbibaḥ kâritoyaṁ sabhaktibhiḥ*
sanvatsarai 1080 *Thaṁbaka Pa—*
4. *ppakâbhyâm ghâṭitah. Oṁ.*

"Om! The illustrious Jinadeva (*was*) a Sûri; after him was he who is named the illustrious Bhâvadeva. His pupil (*is*) the Âchârya Vijayasiṅga (*Vijayasiṁha*). Exhorted by him the virtuous laymen, who reside in Navagrâma, Sthâna, and other (*towns*), caused to be made, full of devotion, (*and*) in accordance with their means, this fourfold Vardhamâna; it was fashioned in the (*Vikrama*) year 1080 by Thambhaka and Pappaka. Om!"[2]

---

[1] "Epigraphia Indica," Vol. II, p. 200, No. XXXVII. See Boyer, "L' Époque de Kaniska" (*J. as.* maiguin, 1900, pp. 571—575). The translation in the text has accidentally omitted the words "out of the Sirigriha *saṁbhoga*." The inscription dates from the early years of Kanishka.

[2] "Epigraphia Indica," Vol. II, p. 211, No. XLI.

The characters, as Bühler observes, admit of no doubt as to the era used. The day of the week or month not being specified, the exact equivalent date A. D. cannot be determined. But the year may be taken as A. D. 1023. The date was probably expressed in the northern fashion, that is to say, according to a year in which the month ends with the full moon. The exact equivalent year depends on the circumstance whether the writer counted 1080 years as expired, or the ten hundred and eightieth year as current. Both modes of reckoning were in use.

The inscription was recorded within about five years of the sack of Mathurâ by Mahmûd of Ghaznî in A. D. 1018, when the temples are said to have been burnt. It would seem that the Jain temples on the Kankâlî mound must have escaped destruction.

PLATE XCI.

MATHURA SERIES.—KANKĀLĪ TĪLĀ.

ANCIENT IMAGES OF VARDHAMĀNA.

SCALE

INCHES 12 9 6 3 0 1 FOOT

Photo-lithographed at the Survey of India Offices, Calcutta, October [illegible]

CHAPTER XIX.—VARDHAMANA.

PLATE XCI.

TWO IMAGES OF VARDHAMÂṆA.

THE statues figured in this plate are identified as being representations of Vardhamâṇa by the lions in the pedestals. The defaced inscription in early characters of the right hand figure begins with the word *namo,* "homage." That figure is seated under his sacred tree. One of his attendants is a Nâga, with a canopy of cobra hoods. The other image is seated under a small canopy. Both figures are attended by angels, or *Gandharvas,* hovering in the air and offering garlands.

PLATE XCII.

LIFE-SIZE IMAGE OF A SEATED JINA.

The loss of the pedestal, on which the distinctive symbol would have been carved, makes it impossible to say which of the twenty-four Tirthaṁkaras is here represented.

The aureole is a fine and elaborate piece of work. The deeply undercut foliage in the band of sculpture surrounding the rays proceeding from the head indicates that the statue was executed while art still flourished, probably during the Kushân period.

It is believed that this image was not found in the Kankâli mound, but the exact findspot is uncertain.

MATHURA SERIES.—KANKÂLÎ TÎLÂ.

LIFE-SIZE IMAGE OF SEATED JINA.

SCALE OF FEET

INCHES 12 ∴ 1 2 FEET

Photo-zincographed at the Survey of India Offices, Calcutta, October 188[illegible].

MATHURA SERIES.—KANKÂLÎ TÎLÂ.

SMALL IMAGE OF SEATED VARDHAMÂNA.

SCALE.

INCHES 12 9 6 3 1 FOOT

Photo-autographed at the Survey of India Offices, Calcutta, October 1898.

PLATE XCIII.

SEATED IMAGE OF VARDHAMÂṆA.

This work seems to belong to approximately the same period as that last described. The lions on the pedestal indicate that the saint represented is Vardhamâṇa.

Between the lions two kneeling worshippers adore a sacred wheel with thirteen spokes. The rays of the aureole are in the form of leaves, and are surrounded by elaborately-carved bands and mouldings.

The saint sits in front of a *toraṇa* gateway, parts of which are shown.

The traces of an inscription are illegible.

PLATE XCIV.

VARDHAMÂṆA, SURROUNDED BY THE PREVIOUS 23 TÎRTHAṀKARAS.

The saint is represented seated in the usual attitude of meditation *(dhyânamudrâ)*, on a cushion. The lions in the pedestal show that Vardhamâṇa or Mahâvîra is the person represented. His 23 predecessors in miniature are arranged as a border, seven at the top and eight at each side.

The arrangement of the hair of the principal figure is in rolls, nearly as in Plate XC, figure 1, and not in conventional curls as in Plates XCII, XCIII, XCV, and XCVI. The form of the upper canopy is also unusual, and is perhaps intended for a conventional tree.

The inscription on the pedestal is unfortunately very imperfect. It includes the word *pratimâ*, "image." The characters may date from the fifth century A. D. So far as I can ascertain, this record has not been edited. The slab was discovered in the season 1889-90.

MATHURA SERIES.—KANKÂLÎ TÎLÂ.

IMAGE OF VARDHAMÂNA SURROUNDED BY THE PREVIOUS 23 TIRTHAMKARAS.

SCALE

INCHES 12 6 0 1 FOOT

Photo-zincographed at the Survey of India Offices, Calcutta. October [illegible]

MATHURA SERIES.—KANKÂLÎ TÎLÂ

COLOSSAL IMAGE OF SEATED TIRTHAMKARA, DATED SAMVAT 1134.

SCALE OF FEET

INCHES 12 6 0 1 2 FEET

Photo-zincographed at the Survey of India Offices, Calcutta, October 18[illegible]

PLATE XCV.

MATHURA SERIES.—KANKÂLÎ TÎLÂ.

COLOSSAL IMAGE OF SEATED TIRTHAMKARA, DATED SAMVAT 1038.

Photo-zincographed at the Survey of India Offices, Calcutta, October

CHAPTER XX.—COLOSSAL JAIN IMAGES.

PLATES XCV AND XCVI.

COLOSSAL IMAGES OF SEATED TÎRTHAMKARAS, DATED SAMVAT 1038 AND 1134.

THESE statues are remarkable only for their dates, Vikrama Samvat 1038, equivalent to A. D. 981, and Vikrama Samvat 1134, equivalent to A. D. 1077. The inscriptions, according to Dr. Führer, state that the dedications were made by the Śvetâmbara community of Mathurâ.[1]

The image dated V. S. 1080, A. D. 1023, previously described (Plate XC, figure 3), was dedicated by the Digambara sect, and was found near their temple to the west. These two colossal images dated 1038 and 1134 were found in December 1889 near the more central temple, which seems to have belonged to the Śvetâmbara sect.

Photographs of them were taken at the time of the discovery by local artists, Chunni Lal and Bhawani Ram, who also photographed from the well a general view of the excavations, in which both statues are shown.

The sack of Mathurâ by Mahmûd of Ghazni took place in A. D. 1018. One of these images was set up before, and the other nearly sixty years after that event. Whatever may have been the exact amount of destruction wrought by the invader, it is clear that the Jains continued to occupy their holy places with little interruption.

[1] "Progress Report" for 1890-91, p. 16

PLATE XCVII.

PEDESTALS OF COLOSSAL JAIN IMAGES.

The pedestals in this plate are very similar to those of the colossal statues figured in Plates XCV and XCVI. The upper pedestal bears a mediæval inscription which is not legible in the plate. The details of the ornament do not present any feature of special interest.

MATHURA SERIES.—KANKÂLÎ TÎLÂ.

Details of Carving on Pedestals of colossal Images of seated Tírthamkaras.

Fig. 1.

Fig. 2

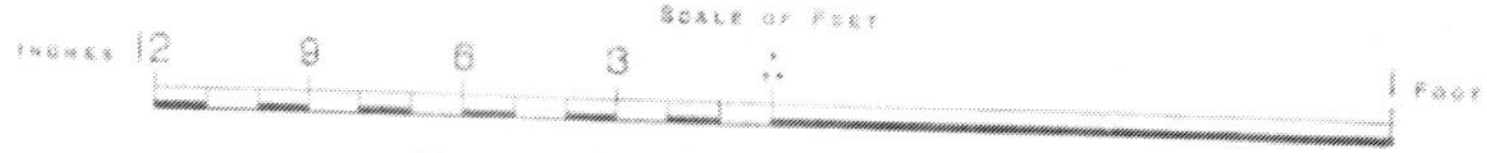

Photo-zincographed at the Survey of India Offices, Calcutta, October [illegible]

MATHURA SERIES.—KANKÂLÎ TÎLÂ.

ANCIENT IMAGE OF RISHABHA, THE FIRST TÎRTHAMKARA.

SCALE OF FOOT

INCHES 12 9 6 3 1 FOOT

Photo-zincographed at the Survey of India Offices, Calcutta, October 189[illegible]

CHAPTER XXI.—RISHABHANATH AND SARASVATI.

PLATE XCVIII

IMAGE OF ṚISHABHANÂTH OR ÂDINÂTH, THE FIRST TÎRTHAṀKARA.

THIS elaborate sculpture, found in the Kankâlî mound in February 1890, is unfortunately much mutilated. The head of the principal figure has been lost, and of the inscription on the pedestal nothing remains but faint traces. The characters seem to be of early form. The attendant figures, male and female, are unusually numerous, and seem to include deities of the Hindu pantheon. The supporters of the pedestal (*siṁhâsana*) are lions, as in Plates XCI and XCIII. But in the sculptures figured in those plates the lions are alone, and thus indicate that the Jina represented is Vardhamâṇa. In this case the presence of two diminutive bulls between the lions indicates that the personage honoured is Ṛishabhanâth, "the Bull-lord."

Statues of Ṛishabhanâth are not common in Northern India.

PLATE XCIX.

STATUES OF SARASVATÎ AND A FEMALE.

THESE two mutilated female statues are among the most curious and interesting of the collection.

The figure on the left side of the plate shows the lower half of a standing woman holding in her left hand in the conventional way a folded sheet. She wears bracelets and anklets and a broad ornamental girdle tied with a string. It is not quite clear whether the legs are intended to appear naked or clothed. The pendant string of the waistband bears an inscription in two lines. The characters are archaic and bear a general resemblance to those used in the time of the Satrap Śodâsa, but some of them are strange to me, and I am unable to decipher them. They are 17 in number, and, so far as I can make them out, I read them as follows :—

Line 1.	1	2	3	4	5	6 —	7	8	9	10
	Ṛi (? *Â*)	*sa*	*bo* (? *bra*) (? *bu*)	*lâ*	*ya*	*dâ* (? *da*) (? *di*)	*na* (? *ne*)	?	*m*	?
Line 2.	11	12	13	14	15	16	17			
	re (?)	*hi* (*he* ?)	*ka*	? (*dâ* ?)	?	*ye*	*yo* (?) (10 ?)			

The first letter is clearly a form of the vowel *a*, and may be read as *â*; but I am inclined to think that it is intended for the vowel *ṛi*. The first word seems to be a proper name in the genitive, and the second word seems to be *dânam* "gift." But what the meaning may be of the strange marks on each side of the *m* (Nos. 8 and 10) I cannot tell.

Character No. 15 looks like the numeral 9, and character No. 13 might be either *ka* or 4. Perhaps this second line records a date.

The right hand figure represents a headless statue of Sarasvatî, the goddess of speech and learning, found in 1889 near the first or eastern temple in the mound, which seems to have belonged to the Śvetâmbara sect.

The goddess is shown sitting squatted, with her knees up, on a rectangular pedestal, holding a manuscript in her left hand. The right hand, which was raised, has been lost. The figure is clothed in very stiffly executed drapery, a small attendant with hair dressed in rolls stands on each side. The attendant on the left wears a tunic and holds a jar—the attendant on the right has his hands clasped in adoration.

The inscription on the pedestal is in seven lines, of which the last is imperfect.

The transliteration and translation by Bühler are as follows :—

Line 1. [Sid]dhaṁ sav LIV [1] himaṁtamâse chaturthe IV divase X [2]a
2. sya purvvâyâṁ Koṭṭiyâto [ga]ṇâto Sthâni[y]âto kulâto
3. Vairâto śâkhâto Śrigṛih[â]to sambhogâto vâchakasyâryya—
4. [H]astahastisya sishyo gaṇisya aryya Mâghahastisya śraddhacharo vâcha kasya a—
5. ryya Devasya nirvarttane Govasya Sihaputrasya lohikakârukasya dânaṁ
6. sarvvasatvânâṁ hitasukhâ eka—Sarasvatî pratishṭhâpitâ avatale raṅgânarttano.
7. me——" [3]

[1] The plate clearly reads XLIV.

[2] The plate seems to read XI or XII.

[3] I doubt if all the letters have been accurately copied in the plate (" Epigraphia Indica," Vol. I, p. 391, No. XXI.)

Details of Ancient Sculptures.

Fragment of ancient female Statue.

Seated Image of Sarasvati, set up in Samvat 54.

Scale of Feet

Inches 12 9 6 3 1 Foot

Photo-lithographed at the Survey of India Offices, Calcutta, October 18[illegible].

"Success! In the year 54 (?), in the fourth, 4, month of winter, on the tenth day, on the (*lunar day specified*) as above, one (*statue of*) Sarasvati, the gift of the smith Gova, son of Siha, (*made*) at the instance of the preacher (*vâchaka*) Aryya-Deva, the *sraddhacharo* of the *gaṇin* Aryya Mâghahasti, the pupil of the preacher Aryya Hastahasti, from the Koṭṭiya *gaṇa*, the Sthâniya *kula*, the Vairâ *śâkhâ*, and the Srigriha *sambhoga* has been set up for the welfare of all beings."

In the *aratala* my stage dancer (?)

In the plate the date clearly reads XLIV, not LIV as doubtfully read by Bühler. This date is probably expressed in terms of the Kushân era.

The record is a good example of a spiritual pedigree, and gives several particulars as to the organization of the Jain church. Images of Sarasvatî are said to be still met with in Jain temples.

CHAPTER XXII.—SUNDRY SCULPTURES.

PLATE C.

SCULPTURED BRACKET OF A *TORAṆA* BEAM.

This plate is here out of place, and should have come earlier in the series, with Plates XXXIV to XXXVII.

The headdresses of the two female figures are curious, and the foliage behind both is admirably executed.

MATHURA SERIES.—KANKÂLÎ TÎLÂ.

FRAGMENT OF DOUBLE SCULPTURED BRACKET SUPPORTING THE VOLUTED END OF TORANA BEAM.

FRONT ELEVATION.

SIDE ELEVATION.

BACK ELEVATION.

SCALE OF FEET

INCHES 12 9 6 3 0 1 FOOT

Photo-zincographed at the Survey of India Offices, Calcutta, October 188[illegible].

MATHURA SERIES.—KANKĀLĪ TĪLA. PLATE CI.

DETAILS OF HEAD-DRESSES.

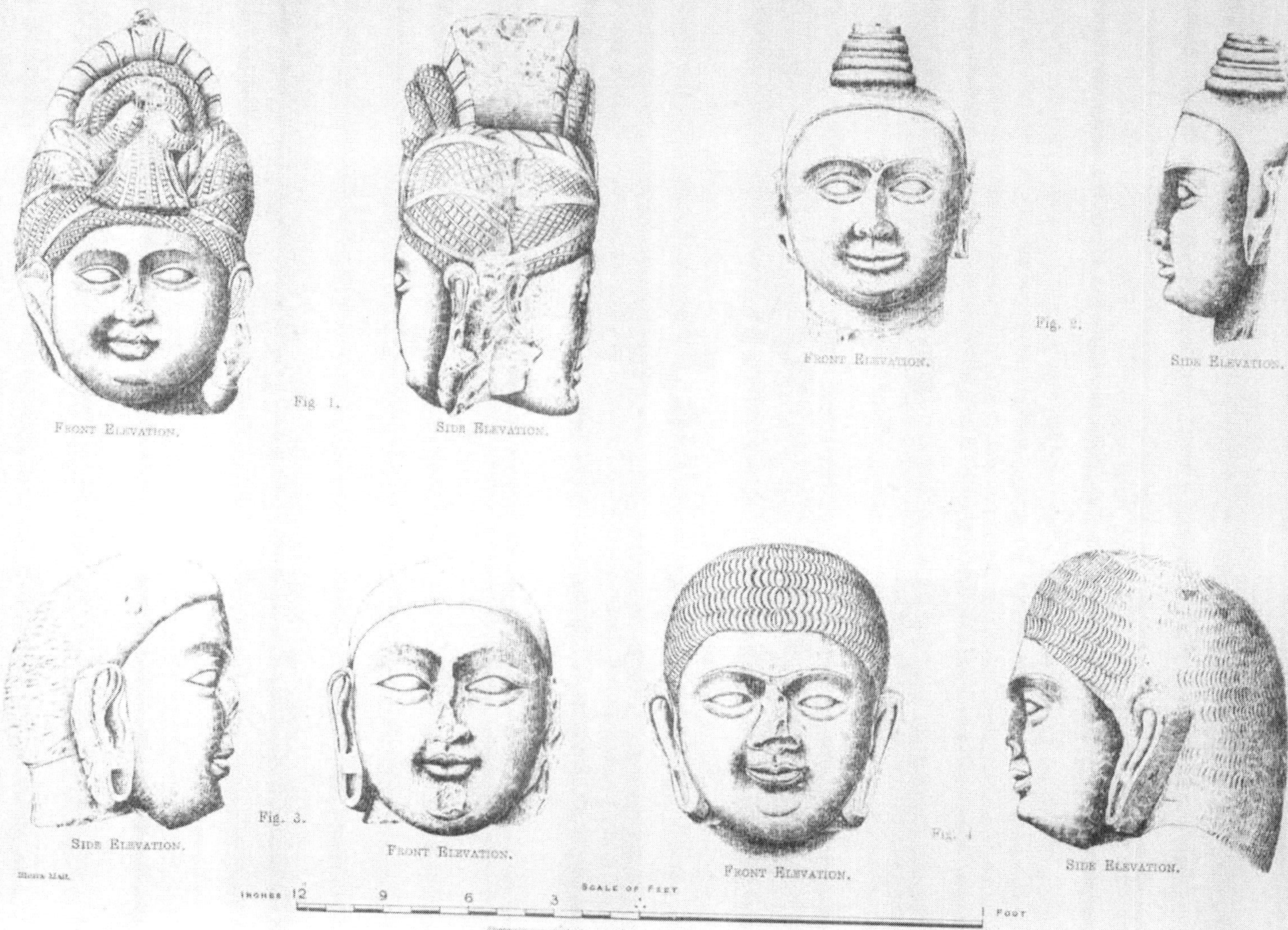

PLATE CI.

HEADS.

THESE heads are of little interest. The various styles of headdress and arrangement of the hair may be noticed.

PLATE CII.

DOUBLE-FACED RIDER ON BULL.

THIS curious sculpture is said by Dr. Führer to have formed the pinnacle of a gateway. It was found to the north of the Kankâlî mound.

The execution is rude, and the general appearance of the work is archaic. The rider carries in his hand a broken shaft, which might be that either of a spear or a trident. Mr. Mukherji suggests that the figure may be an image of Śiva or Mahâdeo. It is possible that this explanation may be correct, even if the sculpture belonged to a Jain edifice, for the Jains do not ignore the existence of the Hindû gods.

MATHURA SERIES.—KANKÂLÎ TÎLÂ.

Pinnacle of Gateway, representing a double-faced Bull-rider.

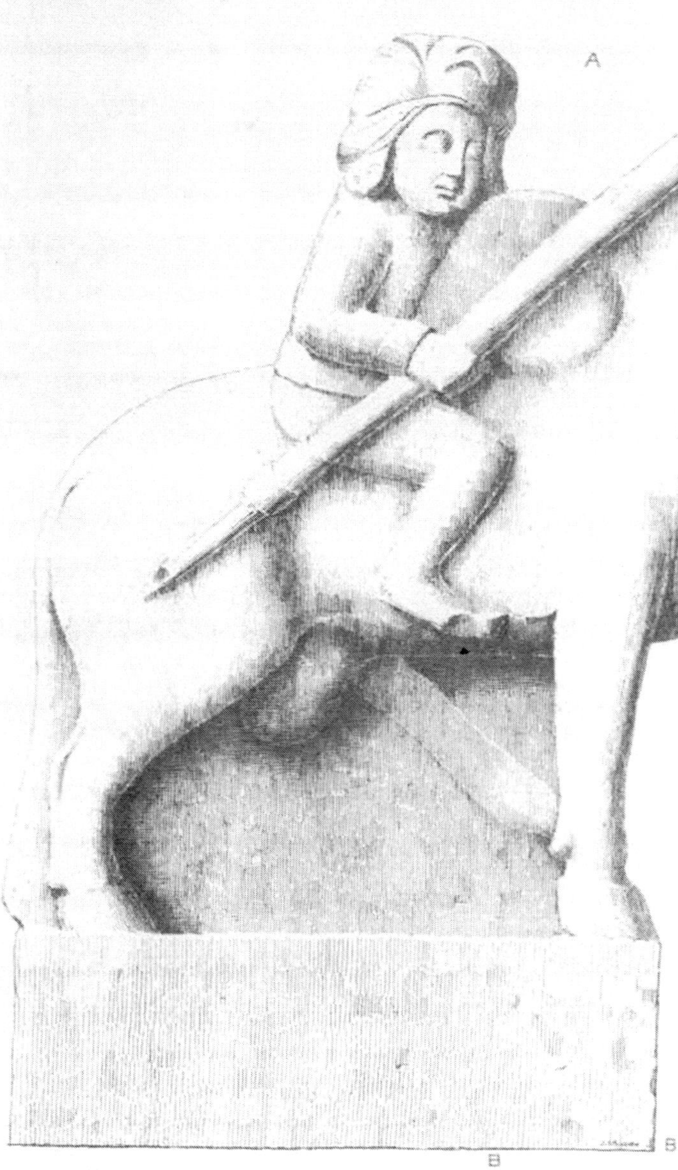

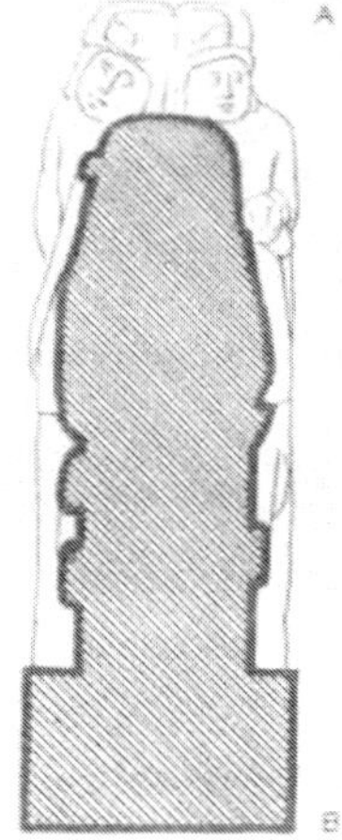

Section.

Scale

Inches 12 9 6 3 0 Foot

Scale of Feet

Inches 12 6 0 1 Foot

Photo-zincographed at the Survey of India Offices, Calcutta, October

MATHURA SERIES. KANKALI TILA.

PLATE [illegible]

Photogravure. Survey of India Offices Calcutta, June 1900.

Inscribed Votive Stupa found near Holi Gate.

CHAPTER XXIII.—SUPPLEMENT.

PLATE CIII.

A JAIN VOTIVE *STÛPA*.

This plate is from a photograph of a small votive *Stûpa* 10½ inches in height found by Mr. Mukherji near the Holi Gate of Mathurâ.

It gives a good idea of what a Jain *Stûpa* was like, and may be compared with Plates XII and XV *ante*.

The inscription opens with the words *Namo arahato Vardhamânasa*, "adoration to the arhat Vardhamâna," in characters similar to those of the Kushân period, or perhaps a little later.

Buhler was under the impression that miniature votive *Stûpas* were not in use by either Buddhists or Jains at an early period, the common Buddhist examples dating from the eighth to the tenth century A. D. [1]

This specimen shows that the use of elaborately-sculptured miniature votive *Stûpas* by the Jains began early.

[1] "A legend of the Jaina *Stûpa* at Mathurâ" (Sitzungsberichte der Kais, Akademie der Wissenschaften. Wien," Band CXXXVII, 1897; reprint, p. 13).

PLATE CIV.

GANEŚA.

This photograph of an image of Ganeśa, seemingly of late date, is of interest as showing that Brahmanical sculptures have been found in the Kankâlî excavations.

MATHURA SERIES – KANKÂLÎ TÎLÂ

PLATE [illegible]

Photo-gravure

Survey of India Offices, Calcutta, July [illegible]

GANESA.

From Kankali Mound

PLATE CVII.

Photogravure

Survey of India Offices, Calcutta, June [illegible]

CAPITAL.

From Dhruva Mound.

MATHURA SERIES — KANKALI TILA.

PLATE [illegible]

Photogravure

Survey of India Offices, Calcutta, June 1900.

CAPITAL

From Dhruva Mound

Photogravure — Survey of India Offices, Calcutta, June 1900

CAPITAL.

From Dhruva Mound.

PLATES CV, CVI, AND CVII.

A CAPITAL.

These plates illustrate a fine capital of unique design, apparently Buddhist, found at the Dhruva Ṭîlâ, or mound, near Mathurâ.

One of the figures seems to be that of the Dying Buddha.